ACCLAIM FOR WILLIAM F. CRAIG
INVENTING ONESELF

"Inventing Oneself is an enjoyable read.
The author has a comfortable manner of telling you a story.
It feels like you are inviting the reader into a personal conversation."
—Father Peter M. Donohue,
President of Villanova University

"Inventing Oneself is an interesting perspective of the S&L crisis combined with a compelling autobiographical account of William F. Craig ... a man with a unique personal journey."
— Tucker Carlson,
Host of Fox News - *Tucker Carlson Tonight*

"More than a business memoir, *Inventing Oneself* is an account of a leading banker, bold entrepreneur and deeply religious family man. Bill Craig's impressive journey is an inspiring case study for all ages, highlighting his principles, resilience and consummate networking."
— Charlie H. Moore Jr.,
Olympian, retired CEO and author of *Running on Purpose*

"Inventing Oneself is a book that artfully weaves through an extraordinary array of issues, events and personalities. The story is not just about business success and challenges but also tackles the joys and heartbreak of family life. At the center of the story is a man who has done much for others and has been justly rewarded.

Bill Craig was lucky to be born into a family of loving immigrants who came to the U.S. from Ireland in 1913 to find a new life. His mother and father raised three sons, who were all born in the Philadelphia area. Bill's father was a chauffeur for a very wealthy family. He was asked to come to Maine each summer with his wife and children. Bill and his brothers had the opportunity to experience the beauty and fun of the Maine coast, an experience that formed a lasting impression.

Bill attended parochial schools and then Villanova University. He was

...continued

always aware that his goal was to achieve an education that would give him an ability to start a career that would make him self-sufficient. Who would have foreseen that through hard work and a keen intellect and a great personality he would build a large and wonderful family and a wonderful business career?

In a delightful autobiography that spans his 87 years, Bill brings us through his career in the banking industry, first at Irving Trust Company in New York and then Shawmut Bank in Boston. He introduces the complexity of dealing with the utility lending department at Irving Trust and at the same time introduces his growing family, soon to be nine children with his lovely wife Louise.

He moved to Shawmut Bank in 1978 and began to build a vast network of friends throughout Boston and New England.

He introduces Cardinals, governors and business people who will become friends and supporters. He becomes involved with some of the most well-known charities in Boston, weaving his influence widely throughout the city. He draws a vivid picture of the role a president of a bank can play in the life of the city.

He describes the incident when his career came to an end at Shawmut Bank. He had been an outside Director of the Pittston Company, an operator of coal mines. The company was in a major dispute with the United Mine Workers of America. The union could not get to first base with the company and so targeted individual directors and brought pressure on their employers. Shawmut Bank was targeted and pressure brought on the then mayor of Boston and the City Council to withdraw deposits from the bank. Bill did not want to back down from the dispute. He had been one of the longest serving directors - for over 30 years - at Pittston. He did not want the Bank to be hurt. So he chose to resign from the Bank rather than leave the Pittston Board. It was a courageous move that brought him great praise in the greater Boston community.

The book concludes with a very satisfying achievement of his business career. Too young to retire, he organized a novel approach to the FDIC to buy the assets of a number of failed banks in New Hampshire. Bill brought together private funds to make it happen. Bill's group was the successful bidder. Three years later, after the banks were back on a profitable basis, Bill and his group were able to sell the banks at a sizable profit. It was a fitting end to a great career."

— John P. Hamill,
Director - Liberty Mutual Insurance Company

INVENTING ONESELF
Blending Business and Politics

INVENTING ONESELF
Blending Business and Politics

WILLIAM F. CRAIG

ADVENTURE IN DISCOVERY

PUBLISHING

JUPITER, FLORIDA

ACKNOWLEDGEMENTS

This book is dedicated to my wife Bernadette. So much of the credit for this book and the happy life I lead belongs to her. I only regret that the many people whom I mention as mentors and contributors to my success never met her. My greatest joy is that I did.

I would like to express my gratitude and praise to the people who showed confidence in me and offered direction and support. Some of them are here, thankfully, but many have passed on.

Fred Kirby, Charles Adams, Greg Adamian, John Burns, Tom Trigg, John Collins, John LaWare, John Hamill, George Murphy, William Peterson, Arthur Boardman, John Childs, Jim Scanlon, Dennis Berk, M.D., Jessica Miller Craig, Dennis Craig, Jack Craig, Bob Truex, Dr. Joseph Haenn, Imogene F. Haenn, Bob Spillman, Carl Ferenbech, Pat and Gerry McGinley, Bob and Helen Coen, Mark Anton, David Nelson, Bud Bylawski, Pamela Mansbach, Terry Hadley, John Chestnut, Bill Leberfinger, Scott Williams, Neil Finnegan, John Green, Lou Hamby, Ray Miller, Father Paul O'Brien, James Topping, Deborah Dyer of the Bar Harbor Historical Society, and my children: Bill, Matt, Ricy, Dede, Bonnie, Cathy, Margie, Nancy, and Carrie.

Special thanks go to the team of people who brought forth the product: Teresa Miller, typist, Beth Bruno, editor, Yvonne Addario, publisher, and Loxahatchee Club staff administrators who provided secretarial services: Jeanie Velez, Brooke Romo, and Karen Schloer.

Good luck, Yvonne Addario, "Adventure in Discovery." The publisher's motto applies in my case… "Helping writers take charge of their book's destiny."

Contents

INTRODUCTION

It must have been a great idea when, with limited savings while unemployed, I raised $40,000,000 and created a company in which I retained a 10% interest. The business was sold for $160,000,000 in three years. Not a dollar was borrowed to purchase or operate the company. There must be a story there.

There is a risk in most things we do in life, and most risks are measurable. The degree of risk ranges from dangerous to benign, with many levels in between. One wouldn't buy insurance if the buyer didn't need to cover a risk. The insurer wouldn't write the policy unless as a group all losses were more than covered by premiums and reserves. Experience determines insurance rates.

Bankable risk should be at the lower end of the range — low risk. Unfortunately, competition may weaken credit judgment and allow greater tolerance of risk. Loan officers are often frowned upon when loans are refused, particularly if the same loan is made by the bank down the street.

Banks can raise funds from a variety of sources. The mix of deposits, purchased funds, long-term debt, and equity has a bearing on leveraging risk. If equity capital is 8% of loan assets, then loans must be at least 95% collectible or you're out of business. In school, a 95% grade gives you an A; in banking, the same 95% gives you an F. Economic cycles have a direct bearing on risk patterns. One can gauge the damaging effect of recessions by looking at the banking industry. Time and time again we have witnessed an overextension of bank credit followed by a bust in the commercial real estate market. Overbuilding was the cause of hundreds of bank failures in the early 1990s, when bank capital was wiped out by charge-offs for nonperforming loans.

Traditionally, the Federal Deposit Insurance Corporation (FDIC) protected the depositors of such failed banks by arranging a merger with a larger secure regional bank. However, in 1990 most regional banks were on a Federal Reserve watch list. Even large banks were singled out as being inadequately capitalized as the result of growing nonperforming and criticized loans.

My plan was to invest and raise capital from other private investors to purchase foreclosed banks. At the Washington, D.C. headquarters of the Federal Deposit Insurance Corporation (FDIC) I explained my plan to use personal savings and non-debt commitments. An investment bank would raise any additional funds needed beyond what I could raise from personal relationships.

Individual investors had never before been cleared to bid against selected banks to recapitalize failed institutions insured by the FDIC. How could an individual gain approval to go up against publically owned large banks?

Much of this story relates to proving creditability and winning confidence. As a former Counter Intelligence Corps (CIC) agent, with a Top Secret clearance, I knew that working with the government, my background experience would be important. After a detailed evaluation by Harrison Young, managing director of the FDIC Department of Foreclosure Resolution, notice was given to me that he would submit my proposal to the FDIC chairman, William Seidman. Chairman Seidman agreed that his office would welcome a bid from a group I would form. "Craig, if you didn't show up we'd have to invent you." Chairman Seidman concluded that my background assured him that I might just be able to pull it off. He could see where my support was coming from -- I got the go-ahead.

WILLIAM F. CRAIG

Father at age 20.

BACKGROUND

My father, Dennis Craig, was born in County Donegal, Ireland, in 1896. His family lived on a dairy farm, supplying milk to nearby towns. In addition to cattle, the family raised and trained horses for riding and carriage use. He finished Glenties Elementary School at age 14 in 1910, and in 1913 at age 17 he came to Philadelphia.

Like most immigrants, there was an urge to bond with people having similar backgrounds: religion, county of origin, economic status, age, and social interests. While my dad was naturally attracted to people with similar interests, he loved being around horses; and in the early 1900s the center for equestrian excitement in the Philadelphia area was the Devon Horse Show and the many polo clubs in the area. While he initially served as a clerk at the Acme stores, his weekends were devoted to horse training events.

He was excited about polo and got to know many of the stable managers and trainers. At the same time, he followed events that involved competition in handling carriage horses. Both polo and carriage handling competitions were rich men's sports.

One of the wealthiest Philadelphia families at that time was the McFadden family. George and Barkley McFadden were dedicated polo players. They came to appreciate Dennis Craig as an especially talented young horse trainer and hired him to care for their ponies. Polo requires stamina for both riders and their mounts. Most riders need at least six ponies per match. Records show Dad traveled as far as Florida on private train cars for polo matches.

In 1920, with another adventurous young Irishman, he took a McFadden coach and four-in-hand from Philadelphia to Bar Harbor, Maine. At that time, like Mackinac Island, Michigan, cars were not permitted on Mount Desert Island. I've been told that the coach is currently housed at a Philadelphia museum. Prior to World War I, the McFadden family purchased Pointe d'Acadie, a grand estate built by George Vanderbilt, who also built the Biltmore in Asheville, North Carolina, the largest house built in America.

My mother, Beatrice Gallagher Craig, was also born in 1896 and raised on a farm outside Swinford, County Mayo, Ireland. Her mother was a Sweeney and her father, Andrew Gallagher, had a grocery store and taught school. In 1903 her father died, as did her younger brother, Andrew. In the late 1800s until the early 1900s, disease accounted for the death of half the people of Ireland before they reached the age of 50.

Beatrice had a brother, Bill, who immigrated to the United States in 1909, as did her brother Patrick a year later. They both chose to come to Philadelphia. In 1915, at age 19, my mother immigrated to the United States and settled with her brother Patrick and his wife, Margaret, in Philadelphia. Uncle Pat was a strong athletic leader. He rose in the ranks of the Philadelphia Fire Department to become a captain. Uncle Bill was my godfather. He tired of selling insurance and returned to the family farm in County Mayo, where he married and raised four children. In the mid '50s, two of his daughters came to live with us while they attended a year of high school under an exchange student program. My cousin, Eugene, Uncle Bill's son, has exchanged visits with us here in the US and in Ireland, and I'm impressed that the Gallagher/Sweeney property has been expanded to several hundred acres.

Father and Mother's wedding picture.

Over the years they acquired neighboring land purchased from relatives of people who chose to immigrate to America. My great uncle, Joe Sweeney, once showed me around, pointing out fields purchased from Gene Tunney's parents. I never mentioned to Mr. Tunney, the world undefeated heavyweight boxing champion, that we could have been neighbors. We served together on the Pittston Board of Directors. The Sweeneys and the Gallaghers have lived on that land for over 300 years. (Gene Tunney married Andrew Carnegie's niece.)

Irish immigrants living in Philadelphia and New York held annual county balls. Dennis and Beatrice loved to dance. They met at the Mayo ball, and throughout my growing years they never missed the Mayo or Donegal balls. They married in 1926 and purchased a house on Copley Road in Upper Darby in Delaware County, Pennsylvania.

111 Copley Road was within walking distance to the 69th Street terminal, the end of the line for the Philadelphia elevated subway train (the "EL"). The terminal was also the terminus for the Philadelphia and Western (P&W), which went west through the suburban main line to Norristown.

Trolley and bus service with routes to towns in the west, north, and south of Delaware and Montgomery counties were also terminated at 69th Street. It was a true transportation hub. In 1928, my brother Dennis was born. I was the middle child, born in 1931. Number three son, John, completed the family in 1934. All three of us were early Depression Era children. In spite of the bad economic times, we felt privileged as members of the middle class. In the early 1920s, the McFadden family, being fond of my dad, wanted to keep him on the payroll. The days of horses were over, and he was offered the position of overseeing the family need for cars and drivers. He transitioned into becoming a chauffeur.

His main calling was to drive for the one McFadden sister, Ella Browning, who inherited the big house at Pointe d'Acadie, while maintaining a mansion in Central City, Philadelphia, and a huge country estate in Villanova, Pennsylvania. When sold it became the Agnes Irwin School, and some of the grounds became part of the Villanova campus. My father's job required that he be in the Philadelphia area three quarters of the year and Bar Harbor from June through September. Mrs. Browning provided our family with a four-bedroom carriage house at Pointe d'Acadie from 1928 through 1941.

Pointe d'Acadie

George Vanderbilt was a 25-year-old bachelor when he bought the forty-acre property and built the Pointe d'Acadie house in 1895. Using Philadelphia architect De Grasse Fox, he built a fashionable shingle-style cottage with multiple bays. He had the Central Park landscape architect, Frederick Law Olmsted, renovate the grounds. Pointe d'Acadie was a humble retreat on the Vanderbilt scale. George's other project, undertaken simultaneously, was not. Biltmore, his estate in Ashville, North Carolina, the largest private residence in the nation, dwarfed even his siblings' Newport, Rhode Island mansions, The Breakers and Marble House.

After George married Edith Stuyvesant in 1898, they expanded Pointe d'Acadie further and spent most summers there with their daughter, Cornelia, until George's death in 1914. In 1920, George McFadden purchased the estate and soon thereafter gave it to his sister, Mrs. Edward Browning. The house was demolished in 1956 due to extremely high upkeep costs. No longer could large estate owners keep gardeners and household staff at $5.00 a day.

Pointe d'Acadie

Ella McFadden married Edward Browning in 1919. He was a medical doctor whose family's wealth came from Pennsylvania coal mining. He died before I was born.

Mrs. Browning's lifestyle was sustained with steady income from McFadden trust accounts. She even sailed through the Depression years. The McFadden Bros. Co.'s financial success was impressive. They were the largest cotton brokers in the world. They were to cotton what Rockefeller and Pews were to oil, what Ford was to automobiles, what DuPont was to chemicals, what Mellon was to banking, what Scott was to paper, what Pulitzer was to newspapers, and what Dorrance was to soup.

All the above tycoons spent their summers on Mount Desert Island, Maine.

Barkley McFadden (Mickey) married Nancy Rockefeller.

For many years, the biggest US export was cotton. The southern cotton growers had the product processed and shipped north to water-powered mills whose products were needed everywhere. McFadden Bros. had sales offices throughout Europe and buying offices in places as far away as Egypt and Vietnam.

Wealthy families named above, and most of the rich people in Bar Harbor with the same names, continue today to be identified and admired for their long-term philanthropy. Mrs. Browning's staff moved with the seasons. I'm most familiar with the crew who maintained Pointe d'Acadie. Carswell was the overseer of the property and lived year-round in a house at the entrance of the back driveway, which was about a half mile long and surrounded by a five-acre garden and six large greenhouses. The greenhouses had coal-fired heaters to sustain fig trees, cutting flowers, potted plants, and grapevines through the winter. Carswell, a Scottish immigrant, had an assistant and three gardeners for cutting the lawns and raking the two half mile gravel driveways each day. One driveway went to the circle in front of the main house and a second back driveway to the service entrance. The property with about 20 acres of lawn was bordered by a mile of ocean headlands and rocky beaches. Pointe d'Acadie would put TV's *Upstairs Downstairs* and *Downton Abbey* to shame.

Dad, Mom, Den, Bill and Jack on the rocks.

The lady of the house had 18 household staff, including: a butler, footman, waitress, cook, kitchen maid, chambermaid, secretary, laundress, chief chef, pastry chef, handyman, yacht captain, assistant mate, chauffeur, plus five full-time gardeners. Every in-house position required wearing a uniform, often morning attire switched to more formal dress in the evening. For the service group, lunch and dinner parties were frequent, hosting a constant flow of visiting guests.

Brother Dennis and Bill on the dock at Pointe d'Acadie.

Upper Darby

While a lot of the glamour about growing up was associated with time at Bar Harbor, the most important formative years were spent at 111 Copley Road, Upper Darby, Pennsylvania. Copley Road was a tree-shaded street with sidewalks on both sides. The houses were semi-detached, made of stone and stucco. The side yards were 20 feet across. There were back alleys, providing access to single car garages and kitchen deliveries. There were hundreds of similar homes nearby, built in the '20s at about the time the 69th Street bus and railroad terminal was completed. The location was ideal for public transportation to stores and schools.

The common floor plan of houses throughout the neighborhood was three bedrooms, two baths, living room with fireplace, separate dining room and kitchen, a full basement with laundry room, and a back lawn access door leading to a one-car garage. The most distinguishing feature was the glass-enclosed front porch.

Most homes were heated with coal furnaces. The byproduct was ash. At least once a week a municipal truck would swing up the alley to empty the ash cans. Kitchen window signs would separately signal for bread, butter and eggs, milk and ice. The iceman with a shoulder rubber apron would daily mount the back stairs to the kitchen carrying a 40-pound block of ice. This steady stream of commercial traffic was occasionally interrupted by the bell ringers. The two most welcome ones were the joyful sound of the ice cream vendor and the special treat of the knife sharpening man with his playful monkey.

In the fall there was a front yard ritual. Fallen leaves would be swept to the pavement curb in piles for jumping and for fires after dark. Today the EPA would have us arrested for burning leaves and for smoke blowing from houses burning coal.

Dennis, Jack and Bill, "Can't wait for long pants!"

A block down the street was St. Alice School, church, convent, and playground on four acres of lawn. St. Alice Parish was the center of my life from kindergarten through eighth grade. The school location was so close that I would walk home for lunch. The church was where I was christened, confirmed, received first communion, and went to frequent confession. I was a choirboy, altar boy, Boy Scout, and played on the football, basketball, and baseball teams. At the time, Latin throughout the Catholic world was sung by the choir and prayed at Mass. As a choirboy and altar boy, I was trained to be clear, but I lacked understanding of many of the Latin phrases.

Holding the cross in a procession.

Without a doubt, I was the best-dressed choirboy and altar boy at St. Alice Church. My mother insisted on pleating every surplice I wore to church services.

She wouldn't let me out the door without an even part in my hair. She attended Mass every day and was strict about school effort. She insisted upon finishing homework prior to playing games. We had endless sessions reciting questions and answers from the catechism. My father was a math whiz and very helpful even through high school. In those early school years, I sometimes wanted to avoid my parents because at the drop of a hat they would ask me to spell a word or answer a math question. St. Alice Parish used one large stone building for church, school, and the events hall. The school was on the top floor, the church on the second floor, and the hall on the first floor. The school had 12 classrooms: Grades 1 through 5 included both boys and girls; in Grades 6, 7, and 8, boys and girls were taught in separate classrooms. Between ages 6 and 13, most of my life was spent in that building or on the fields surrounding it.

Every class was taught by a nun. There were 14 nuns living in a large, beautiful convent on the property. After school one day, I was walking past the convent back door when a nun, who was the convent cook, handed me a sack, and said, "Billy, take this basket of trash to the above-ground stone incinerator."

Upon returning the basket, the nun offered a baked apple as a reward. Some reward! I thanked her, saying I wasn't hungry, but she insisted. I didn't want it. She went on about people starving and remarked that I should sit on the doorstep and eat it. It became dark before she returned to take the dish from my lap. The plate still held the uneaten apple. I heard her grumble something about willful waste. It was a long while before I enjoyed a baked apple. The lesson was, "Nothing is gained by being stubborn." I hope the nun got the lesson; I did.

Many grammar school memories relate to classroom adventures, sports incidents, and social highs and lows. In sixth grade, the state dictated the need for an IQ test. Sister Ursalina was my teacher. The test was in three parts, each timed for twenty minutes. At the end of part one, I needed to go to the bathroom; my bladder needed to be relieved.

"Sister, may I be excused?" I asked.

"No, Billy, this is a timed test. Hold on."

Throughout the second phase, my feet were tapping, and when the papers were distributed for the third phase, I raised my hand and declared that I had finished the test and darted to the bathroom.

Billy F. Craig
Mother's advice: "If you want to look smart, listen more and talk less."

When the IQ results came back to St. Alice School, Sister Ursalina had the entire class line up along the wall to be reseated front to back according to test ranking. The kids who scored high were seated up front. By the time my name was called, my bench was in the back of the room.

We were dismissed for lunch, and as I passed by Sister Ursalina I gloomily asked if I could ever qualify for high school.

I accepted being alone quite a bit. I wasn't bored; I just read more than most kids. I was trying to emulate my brother Den, who always had at least two library books under his bed. In high school, we both took to journalism, writing for the school paper and editing the yearbook. I tried to be thoughtful, but too often I was dependent on humor to be noticed.

I loved Saturday matinée movies, the musicals, and the serials filled with death defying strange looking actors, cowboys, and Indians, preceded by singing the national anthem, sports shorts, cartoons, and world news. If you were under 12 you got the whole show for 15 cents. Every Saturday there were two or three neighborhood kids off to the movies. There were three movie theaters within walking distance.

My mother frowned upon the weekly movie routine. She would say, "Sitting for three hours might become a habit for some kids, but to do it one has to give up Boy Scouts activities and sports."

"But, Mom, other mothers think it's okay."

"Billy, what other mothers do is no concern of mine."

This brings to mind other repeated gems offered by Mom.

"If you don't need it, give it away."

"If it's broke, fix it. If you can't fix it, throw it out."

"Finish your food. They're starving in Europe."

"Time is precious, so don't waste it."

"Make a commitment to finish things."

"If you want to look smart, listen more and talk less."

"How many a man has thrown up his hands at a time when a little more patience would achieve success?"

Relative to that last piece of motherly advice, I was intrigued by a newspaper challenge from Planters Peanuts. How many words can you identify using letters in the company name? The winner would get a new Hudson car. I figured that no one would have enough free time to check out every word that could be found in the English language.

For a whole month that summer, I spent every day studying the complete dictionary in the reference room of the Upper Darby Municipal Library, located just a short walk from home.

I didn't realize at the time, but I was committed to reading and understanding every word in the dictionary.

Well, the family never got the Hudson car, but I surely extended my vocabulary. To this day, I feel the winner must have had a much neater, probably typed presentation; however, it was not wasted time on my part. And I did see it through to the finish.

Character Forming Years

Perhaps it is foolish to consider the first ten years of a child's life to be character forming years. Observations, even at that age, can form lasting opinions. One at any age could not escape observations formed every day surrounded by economic depression and how it affected family life. Depression is most often referred to as an economic condition. But the day-in day-out drift of neighbors and friends into poverty makes the term "depression" relevant to the condition of living.

I remember many people worse off at the time than we were.

They were very often referred to as bums— an unfair term. These were unfortunate young men seeking work from town to town. We were told to clean our plates and not waste food. It became meaningful when we saw a mother feeding beggars who were sitting on the top steps below the kitchen door. There was a steady stream of commerce in our back alley of trash collectors and trash pickers. The trash pickers usually leased a horse and wagon and came out from the city hoping to find something of value in what people threw away.

Unlike today, in the '40s sports were mostly unstructured. Kids recognized talent on the playground. There was no formal supervision. When kids came to play, they knew the routine. You needed to choose up two opposing teams. Usually the most talented players were expected to organize two teams by making alternate selections from the gang present. The better players were chosen first and those not picked respected the common process without complaint. If you wanted to be picked, get better. I sat out many an afternoon. It was an easy lesson to learn. To get off the bench, average wasn't good enough. Those picked early were aggressive but supportive, and practice moved them up the ranks. This idea from the playground laid a foundation for a lifetime of development.

"You can't make it on privilege alone."

Today, parents and adult volunteers make sure every kid gets in the game regardless of talent level. If a team sport has a uniform, your son or daughter should be issued one whether good or bad.

INVENTING ONESELF

THE WAR YEARS (1942-1945)

Everyone my age can remember where and how they heard about the bombing of Pearl Harbor. In 1941, I was 10 years old. On Sunday, December 7th, while waiting to be called to dinner, I was seated comfortably in the living room and scanning a comic book while listening to the *Hit Parade* on the radio. The program was interrupted with an announcement that Pearl Harbor had been bombed by the Japanese.

Soon after, President Roosevelt called it a "Day of Infamy" and asked Congress to declare War. The war years were difficult for most adults. Millions of men were drafted into the services. The economic might of the country shifted to military production needs. Patriotism was running in high gear. Billions of personal savings flowed into war bonds. Income taxes on the wealthy went as high as 92%.

Without complaint, most people accepted gas and food rationing. Kids like me at an early age were sheltered. We expected to knock off the Japanese in short order. After the battle of Midway, it looked like Japan would fall in no time. In Europe we were defending England and supporting Russia. Newspaper reports from around the world were followed daily with printed maps. Progress seemed slow in the early war years. People wondered why we were aiding Churchill with so many troops in North Africa. There was anxiety about a European invasion.

Japan was our war. It turned out that a quick victory in the Pacific theater was overly optimistic. The US Navy and Marines suffered staggering losses in human lives from invading Japanese occupied islands. There were four gold-star mother emblems in house front windows along our short 100-block of Copley Road.

Every street had an air raid committee with a huge box shaped like an oversized coffin, which contained battery-powered flashlights, buckets of sand, hoses, and lots of tools. With all this preparation, you can be sure there were plenty of air raid alerts and blackouts.

At 10 years old, I didn't realize the war's economic effect on our family. It never crossed my mind that Dad no longer had a job, due to gas rationing. I soon learned that he was committed to winning the war by building ships.

Sun Oil Co. (Sunoco), owned by the Pew family, included Sun Ship Building Co., which became dedicated to keeping seaborne transport ahead of the German U-boat damage. My father signed up to do whatever he could to support the war effort. I couldn't fathom what a job on the launching gang at Sun Shipyard was about. I only knew with pride that my dad was into the war effort.

A bus in the early morning took my father from the 69th Street terminal to Sun Shipyard at Chester, Pennsylvania, on the Delaware River. Ship building in the US during World War II was more important than many historians give credit. The German U-boats were decimating the US supply to Britain. Convoys were sitting ducks, and we as a country were racing to refill losses at sea. At Sun Ship, cargo vessels and tankers were being launched at a spectacular rate of one every three weeks.

Corporate management was excellent. Every segment of mass production demonstrated remarkable skills. A ship must be built in dry dock or on modestly sloping rails. When the ship is launched, it slides on the steel rails into the deep river water. During construction, the hull must be supported from the bottom up with 14-inch by 16-inch blocks of wood, 12 feet apart. All hull construction work is supported by these wood blocks, allowing what is called the launching way. When it comes to launch time, a team of men, who placed the supports, must knock them out with sledges and mallets. That's the job of the launching gang.

The Red Wagon

Reflecting on the war years brings to mind events associated with going from 10 to 15 years old in 1946. A quick review brings to mind: piano lessons; party-line telephone (we had two rings, but you could still listen to another party's calls); new outfits at Easter; and going from short pants to knickers to long trousers with a shirt and tie. A fond memory was finding a red wagon when camping out in the woods.

In 1943, at age 12, on a weekend camping trip to a wooded area called Menoa Falls, I spotted a metal red wagon stuck in the bushes. Friends reported that it had been there for weeks. After a fortnight, at 5:30 am, I hopped on a Red Arrow trolley and headed out 10 miles on West Chester Pike. I hiked three miles down a country road, waded over the dam, and after two weeks the prize was still hidden in the bushes. Pulling the little red wagon clear and hauling it back to West Chester Pike, I was delighted to discover that the road back home was mostly downhill. With a knee in the wagon and a hand holding the handle, I managed to get to school by 8:30.

The red wagon was my first step to financial independence. On top of the hill at 69th Street was the Penn Fruit store. It was where most people in the nearby neighborhoods shopped for groceries. Because public transportation was so convenient and gas was rationed, most people walked to the store. However, carrying food purchases in bags and boxes was a problem. I became the solution.

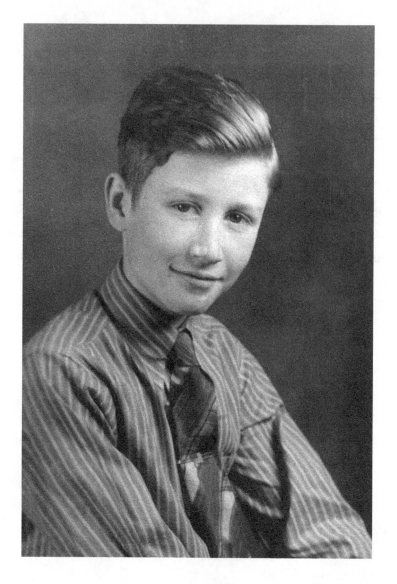

Billy got a red wagon.

With my little red wagon, I would unburden the shopper and follow right behind her for several blocks until the goods were deposited on the kitchen counter. I provided this service for a tip of 15 or 20 cents. Often, especially on Saturdays, there would be half a dozen kids my age seeking out shoppers looking for help. Many women picked me because they knew my mother. Often though, I would seek an advantage by slipping behind the checkout counters in search of someone pushing a full cart. On Sundays I sold newspapers in front of St. Alice Church, and on Wednesdays I delivered the *Upper Darby News*. Thanks to my little red wagon, I never needed to beg for movie money again.

High School

In May 1945, at 14, I finished grade 8 at St. Alice School. The following September I started high school at West Philadelphia Catholic High School for Boys, located at 49th and Chestnut Streets in Philadelphia. The faculty was primarily Christian Brothers of the St. John Baptist de LaSalle Order. The commute took 45 minutes each way. The ride on the elevated train to 52nd Street took less than half an hour and there was a short walk on both ends of the trip. While in grade school, having had the privilege of lunch at home, it was a big adjustment to become a "brown bagger." Sandwiches wrapped in wax paper and a piece of fruit with a cookie was the lunch I carried from home. Sliced white bread dabbed with butter would never be suitable with tomato and lettuce if the assigned lunchtime was after 11 am. Most sandwiches were made with bologna, cheese, salami, spam, other cold cuts, or the frequent peanut butter and jelly.

In my high school freshman year, I contracted rheumatic fever and was bedridden for three months. It was so painful I couldn't walk. I didn't want anyone to touch the bed. All I could do was listen to soaps on the radio and play board games while lying in bed. The best sound was hearing my father's footsteps coming up the stairs to my room to play poker, chess, or checkers.

When I was able to return to high school, I was under strict doctor's orders to be especially careful about climbing stairs.

There was fear that pushing recovery might bring on heart damage. Since my daily high school travel routine called for climbing a hundred stairs to the elevated train platform at 52nd Street, it often happened that several trains would pass before I got to the top.

Patience paid off. By my junior year, the health worry had passed. No heart murmur was detected, and in the spring of that year I ran in the Penn relays. High school, in retrospect, flashed by. I won a trophy in bowling, but try as I might I wasn't up to making the school basketball team.

In 1949, my senior year, the regional high school basketball championship was between West Catholic and Overbrook High. The feeling was desperate. We had Ernie Beck, who went on to captain the University of Pennsylvania team. Overbrook had Wilt Chamberlain, the seven-foot tall center who years later was inducted into the NBA Hall of Fame. All the boys at West were exuberant when our team won the game.

My most dreaded courses in high school were in foreign languages. The first two years were for credits in Spanish, and the second two years were for German. Spanish had a lot of Latin derivatives, and I had a carryover from grade school. German was another matter, with Brother Egbert, a native German. He felt it was his responsibility to make us conversational Germans. He was demonstrably excitable at the blackboard, snapping chalk, frustrated by the class response.

My senior year was full of college preparation courses.

While in high school, I dated Joan Donahue, who lived in the 200 block of Copley Road. Her father owned the local Catholic undertaker business. She was very pretty, very smart, the same age and blond. We went sledding together on local hilly streets that escaped being cindered and played tennis at a nearby township facility. She attended Sharon Hill Academy and invited me to escort her to school dances. Sharon Hill Academy was located in Drexel Hill, Upper Darby, with trolley access from the 69th Street terminal. Since I was not old enough to drive, we took the trolley to a semi-formal dance at her school. The trolley tracks ran down the center of the highway across from her school. Joan, in a long gown at 15 years old, behaved like a lady, while her escort darted across the highway, leaving her on the trolley platform. I'll never forget how stupid I felt later, wondering where my first romance might have gone if I hadn't been such a jerk. *Lesson learned*, I thought.

I was taken aback when I learned years later that she became an office secretary for my future father-in-law, Dr. Joseph Haenn at Haenn Lumber Co.

End of World War II

VE (Victory in Europe) Day, May 8, 1945, marked the end of fighting in Europe. It was a day of celebration throughout the US. I'll never forget the evening of the official announcement. Accompanied by two classmates, we rode the EL train into Center City Philadelphia. Groups formed unofficial parades, bugles blared, people danced in the streets, confetti flew, and fireworks echoed around the tall office buildings. Anyone in uniform got hugs and kisses. We were wide-eyed 14-year-olds enjoying all the excitement. 1945 was a year to remember. In addition to VE Day, it was the year President Roosevelt died and the year I graduated from grammar school.

Harry Truman succeeded Roosevelt and was immediately drawn into negotiations with Stalin and Churchill about world order.

In 1945, the US forces in the Far East were anxiously

anticipating the invasion of the Japanese homeland. Our allies had been focused on Europe. American forces were primarily pushing back against Japan. It was estimated that a Japanese mainland invasion could cost a million lives. Truman was advised that there was a successful atomic bomb explosion at the Manhattan Project desert site in Los Alamos, New Mexico. The power released could destroy a major city. The military chiefs realized the significance of using the bomb and left it to the President to decide. Truman gave the go-ahead, noting a sign on his desk, "The buck stops here."

Hiroshima was hit first with devastation never seen before. When days later a second A-bomb struck Nagasaki, Japan surrendered with a single condition: the Emperor would not be held accountable.

The deal was signed aboard the battleship *USS Missouri*, September 2, 1945. World War II was over. The question was: How could we get back to what anyone remembered as a normal life?

The war effort had taken its toll on civilian life. The financial depression had not ended prior to the war. How could post-war market demand get the country back on its feet?

In the next few years, government stood out for its leadership. Unlike the rest of the world, our infrastructure was not damaged, but the U. S. industrial output was almost entirely designed to support the military effort. In a short time, there was the formation of international political and economic programs. The Bretton Woods Conference, held in New Hampshire, recognized the need to support the gold standard and the formulation of currency exchange standards along with the formation of the World Bank and the IMF. The United Nations was formed, followed by the US introduction of the Marshall Plan to put Europe back on its feet.

President Truman had his hands full implementing agreements the allies made without his input. One of his problems occurred because Stalin believed that the Soviet Union deserved control of more eastern European territory. He felt his cause was justified by the significant loss of life his country had suffered while defending the Eastern Front. Communist Russia had become a diplomatic nightmare. The fear was that Russia was attempting to infiltrate our government by promoting communism in all our influential institutions. Senator Joseph McCarthy promoted hysteria with accusations that Communists had infiltrated the State Department, the Army, and Hollywood. Congressional hearings revealed McCarthy's accusations were overblown.

In the meantime, rationing was lifted, but many consumer products were still in short supply, and hoarding continued until civilian production caught up to demand.

Many eastern European countries prior to the war had unelected rulers. Many of them fled to England during the war. These people were encouraged to become more democratic and encourage the election of officials. With Soviet occupation and influence, these elections frequently brought in communist governments.

Poland, Hungary, Czechoslovakia and the Baltic countries, even Italy, France, Turkey and Greece, had active communist parties seeking to use democratic elections to take control.

The occupation of Germany split Berlin into four zones: Russian, American, British and French. The Russians expanded their authority to control a united West Germany, including their pieces of East Berlin, and began a program to push the US and Britain out of their sectors. President Truman showed stubborn resistance. After the Russians cut off all road and rail access, Truman introduced the Berlin airlift, breaking the embargo.

31

We were not about to roll over for Stalin. The answer was NATO. From the outset, it was a military union of Western Europe and the US: "One for all and all for one." The combined military strength of NATO far exceeded that of the Soviet Union, and Russia could never keep up with US preparedness. The only thing that was considered by Russia as an equalizer was the Russian A-bomb and their missile capability demonstrated by Sputnik. Fortunately, our missile development neutralized their short-term advantage.

Post World War II

World War I marked the downfall of French, German, and English aristocracies. It was a war of choice — a big mistake. The contest was between aristocracies while the underclass paid the price.

One would expect that the devastation and cost both in property and manpower for the winners and losers would have provided more than the slogan "the war to end all wars." The short period between the signing of the armistice in 1919 and the German invasion of neighboring countries in 1939 was an unbelievable 20 years — a period that included 10 years of worldwide depression.

The Sun Shipyard closed shortly after VE Day, and my father, at age 51, was out of work. It was not a good time for a man that age to begin looking to start a new career. He was pleased when Mrs. Browning asked him to return as her chauffeur. Our family was delighted knowing we would be returning to Bar Harbor for the summer. The war years 1942 through 1945 called for food and gasoline rationing. The Bar Harbor houses were shuttered. Without gas for cars, there wasn't a need for a chauffeur. Our family didn't return to Bar Harbor until the summer of 1946.

Pointe d'Acadie projected into Frenchman Bay, which was closely patrolled by the US Coast Guard and the US Navy protecting against espionage. Several Nazi spies were landed by German submarines within a mile of the point.

War preparations were within sight, as the US Navy used Bald Porcupine Island's eastern end for torpedo practice. The island was owned by Mrs. Browning, whose son, Teddy, a friend of FDR, spent the war years in Washington, D.C., as a $1-a-year man responsible for naval personnel equipment purchases. The torpedoes, exploding about a half mile from the Browning estate, created repercussions causing cracks and leaks at the very large first-of-its-kind Vanderbilt swimming pool. One cannot sue the government, but in 1946 the US Senate passed a bill restoring the pool. The pool had been carved out by nature. It was 200 feet long and about 120 feet wide, surrounded by lawn bordered by ferns, edged with white birch intermixed with balsa fir and white pine. With a white sandy bottom, the pool was maintained by being emptied into the adjacent ocean cove at low tide through a gate controlling water flow through a 30-inch pipe. The gate would be closed after the pool emptied, and a team of gardeners would rake the sand bottom smooth. The gate was reopened when the tide was high, and the pool would quickly refill. The pool had a seaside granite block 15-foot wall, separated from the ocean by a narrow beach. The tides in the area rose and fell 12 feet twice a day. The system allowed for the pool water to warm for bathing. It took a week for the pool water to get up to 75°F, while water temperature at the beach averaged 50°F during the summer. The pool was off limits for the help; however, Mrs. Browning encouraged the Craig boys to use the pool in the afternoons. I learned to swim at the indoor heated pool at the Bar Harbor YMCA. Using the Browning pool was a privilege.

There was a pool house with a central high-ceilinged 20-foot x 20-foot beamed living room/dining room with large windows and a massive stone fireplace with a broad chimney. A chill in the air would call for a wood fire fed by evenly cut white birch logs, stacked in a wood box outside the front door. The cabin had walls and a roof covered by cedar shingles. It had six dressing rooms and a stairway to the pool, intercepted halfway by a nicely furnished deck.

Bill's dad in full swimsuit at Pointe d'Acadie pool.

Mrs. Browning invited about 12 friends with notification to swim there. A maid each day would collect the wet swim wear from the lockers, take them to the estate laundry where they would be cleaned, dried, and returned to a closet at the pool house. In June 1946, we were back at the charming coach house on the lovely Browning estate, Pointe d'Acadie. I had to wait until September to get my driver's license. Brother Dennis, at 18, was able to use Dad's car, so it was handy to be dating the Caugh sisters, Barbara and Janis. With the car, we were able to go dancing at the Kimball House in Northeast Harbor on Monday nights and on Wednesdays at the airport hangar off the island at Trenton, Maine.

Both affairs included great local bands. Brother Den, an excellent musician, would often be asked to fill in as a singer, at the piano, or on the drums. He studied piano and violin for many years. While jacket and tie were proper attire for both events, the Kimball House affair was considered more upscale. The hangar was huge with enormous sliding doors, usually open to welcome the summer breeze and starlit sky. It had a highly waxed painted floor. Normally there was an eight-piece band.

This was the big band era, and most numbers resembled arrangements by Jimmy Dorsey, Glenn Miller, Woody Herman, or Harry James. You couldn't control your feet when they played the "Darktown Strutters Ball."

Occasionally the airport was socked in with fog. The field was primarily used for private planes, mostly by well-to-do families living on Mount Desert Island. The runway was not fitted with lights, so the windsock was unseen at night. There was a radio station on the property, but after dark, planes were directed to go to Bangor. Late one evening, while the dance was hopping, an announcement came from the bandstand that a pilot with a fuel problem was circling the field. We were requested to go to our cars, follow the two emergency vehicles, line up on either side of the runway, face the strip with our high beams, and help the pilot land safely. The plane continued to circle, while the pilot watched complete disorder on the ground. Finally, instructions were followed and the plane landed safely.

That summer Den and I crewed for friends at several Bar Harbor Yacht Club sailing races. At that time there was strict prohibition of paid crew. Teachers and coaches were barred from participation in amateur competition. This was still part of the age of strict amateur sport. While most people wouldn't go out of their way to police the edges of this standard, the question was raised whether a math and science tutor was a paid professional. We were on boats that had winning records and an anonymous protest suggested that Den, who was also teaching piano, was an ineligible professional. The challenge was dropped.

The summer of 1946 was most memorable. In July, the battleship USS Missouri (the "Mighty Mo"), with Admiral Todd in command, was anchored next to Bald Porcupine Island, directly across from Pointe d'Acadie, about one mile offshore. The ship was making a victory tour of East Coast cities. Somehow we were included in a group invited to board the ship. A bronze plaque commemorating the signing of the Japanese surrender was bolted on the deck, the spot where the signing took place. I remember reading about the agonizingly heroic invasions of so many Pacific islands by the US Marines. It's hard to believe any enemy could survive pre-invasion bombardment delivered by the awesome power of the USS Missouri's guns. Den was thrilled visiting this star of our Navy fleet, since he would be shipping out as an ensign in three years, having won an ROTC Navy four-year scholarship to Villanova. Mother, Den, Jack, and I returned by train to Philadelphia in early September. We anticipated having Father join us the following month. I couldn't wait for his return to Philadelphia. He was teaching me to drive on Sundays at store parking lots. I needed his support and car to go for my driver's license.

Bar Harbor Forest Fire

Little did we know that 1947 would be the last of Bar Harbor's "golden age." In mid-October, fire spread from the town dump. It had been an extended dry season. The fire moved swiftly through the tender fir and pine forest, destroying everything in its path. That path was directed by the wind, which was out of the west, and it was a godsend that the town center was spared, as were many properties along the coast. However, all the large hotels were burned to the ground in minutes. There had been so much rejoicing that summer to see these hotels reopen having been mothballed throughout the war years. Fortunately, the hotels had closed for the season. In those days it was a practice for hotel guests to stay for a week or month. Bar Harbor was a destination resort; it did not attract traveling tourists. Most of the summer cottage people left the area before the fire, and the hotels had closed. Evacuation of a full summer crowd would have been almost impossible. The only road off the island was Route 3, a two-lane road 20 miles to Ellsworth. The road to Northeast Harbor (nine miles) was in the path of the fire. While the fire took a few buildings on the coast close to town, it spared the downtown area.

It headed off to the high ground, leaping through estates and destroying mansions overlooking the bay. It moved swiftly toward the center of Mount Desert Island, vaporizing the Kebo Valley Golf Club building, the opera house, and on into Acadia National Park. It went straight up Cadillac Mountain, which rises 1,600 feet from the sea; and when the French explorer Champlain sailed by he noticed that the top of the mountain was bare, ground down during the glacier age. The explorer gave the island the name "Mount Desert." The fire burned itself out when it reached the uncovered granite rock near the top of the mountain. The fire never reached Pointe d'Acadie; however, over 60 summer residences were destroyed along with the trees and gardens that beautified those estates. All the celebration that accompanied returning from the war years went up in smoke. Bar Harbor would never be the same. The US Navy and National Guard came to fight remaining pockets of fire and protect property from looting.

My father and Mrs. Browning and staff were in the process of closing Pointe d'Acadie. Dad arranged for all the cars to be taken to the wide-open town baseball field until it was safe to drive to Bangor.

A seasonal resident, Joseph Pulitzer, owner of the *New York Daily News* and the *St Louis Post Dispatch*, and founder of the Pulitzer Prize for Journalism, arranged for the city manager and a staff of consultants to study the problems caused by the disaster. They came up with a solution to the town's washed out tax base. The recommended solution angered many, but most remaining property owners agreed it made sense. Taxes on summer residences that survived would be increased to three times the taxes paid prior to the disaster. This way the year-round residents would avoid having their taxes raised. Their income would most likely suffer due to the loss of summer cottage rental business.

While the lifestyle of the rich was jolted, the townspeople were saved by the national post war social changes, which encouraged the construction of motels, thus significantly increasing tourist visitors. The Rockefeller family added another 10,000 acres to Acadia National Park, including 50 miles of carriage trails available for horses and bikes. The Park Service received an increased budget to replant hardwood trees in several square miles of burned out pines. Bar Harbor was liberal about issuing construction permits to induce financing new hotels and motels.

The first new seasonal motel came about by expanding the former Yacht Club and reading room. It became the 100-room Bar Harbor Motor Motel. Within a year, six other motels were built on former estates with exceptional ocean views. Fortunately, the town's churches, school, and commercial properties were not damaged. The spirit of the town was reflected in a comment made by the mayor: "We can't count on inherited wealth to protect our future. We've been stripped of half of our estate-sourced income. We must welcome tourist visitors while remaining loyal to the surviving wealthy cottage owners."

The Stotesbury estate, owned by a Philadelphia J.P. Morgan partner, was destroyed by the fire. The large property on deep water was cleared and a passenger terminal and dock were constructed to service the Blue Nose Ferry, sailing between Bar Harbor, Maine, and Halifax, Nova Scotia.

INVENTING ONESELF

PEACE TIME ECONOMY

For five years the business of businesses was providing support for the national war effort. US industry was directed by the War Production Board. If you were employed, you probably worked for the government. Your savings were mostly directed toward war bonds, with interest accumulated until maturity. Income taxes ran as high as 92 percent for the top bracket. While some businesses had outstanding revenues, those businesses must now be converted to fulfill peacetime demand. It required new skills and new equipment.

Returning veterans were there to fill many open jobs, but many skills were still in short supply. The GI Bill was a great idea. Veterans were given an upward lift through education to career opportunities they would otherwise miss. The war years brought droves of women into the workplace. With the taste of independence that jobs outside the home gave women, there was no looking back. Women sought more education and training. The returning GIs, having met with fellow soldiers and sailors from all over the country and around the world, were a generation freed from hometown loyalty. The fear of seeking opportunities away from the neighborhood was lifted. Mobility to seek and find opportunity in a much broader marketplace was a positive change for job seekers.

As a country, it was time to junk the icebox for an electric refrigerator. I can clearly remember Ronald Reagan pushing the idea of having a GE fridge. Every car manufacturer came out with a fashionable new model. If you check out the big design changes between the 1941 (pre-war) cars and those in the 1948 market, wow! I wanted one.

The switch from war to peace was not entirely smooth; it was a period of halting yet significant upward movement. After five years when government told both businesses and individuals what to do, people were now free to make choices.

In June 1949, I graduated from West Catholic and took a summer job with the Department of Interior Park Service cleaning trails at Acadia National Park. The US had just entered the Korean War and the draft was resumed. Planning to enter my freshman class at Villanova, I received an exemption.

College Years

Very little changed in my lifestyle between high school and college. While continuing to live at home, I commuted in the opposite direction. Again, my commute to and from school began with a walk to the 69th Street terminal. Rather than ride the EL into the city, I took the Philadelphia & Western (P&W) west to the Villanova campus station.

I still carried a brown bag lunch, joining other commuters sitting at long tables in a converted army Quonset hut called the pie shop. The class average age was influenced by returning older veterans. Tuition by today's standards was quite low ($1,500 per semester). Many students lived off-campus due to a shortage of dorm space. The registration office was swamped by applications for admission. It was noticeable that the class was overbooked. I chose to major in economics and minor in accounting. These were popular choices, and during orientation we heard from an official source that 30 percent of that freshman class would not be around for the second semester.

What an incentive to be attentive and improve study habits.

The warning turned out to be true, as the class size shrank significantly. In spite of the early anxiety, it was a great year socially and academically. My parents felt that since I didn't go away to college, I should look for a summer job away from home. A classmate, Art Menzel, was from Stone Harbor, New Jersey. His parents owned The Shelter Haven Hotel and Fred's bar, restaurant, and liquor store. The complex was only a block from the beach.

Ed Corr, Bill, and Ned Gable on the Stone Harbor Beach.

Three classmates were invited by Menzel to sign up for work at his family business for the summer. We became waiters, busboys, handymen, and painters. We had Sundays and every afternoon off. Like myself, the other two co-workers, Ed Corr and

43

Ned Gable, were from the Philadelphia area and were buddies at Villanova. I shared a room at the hotel with Ned, while Ed lived at his parents' Stone Harbor summer home. Ed owned a boat, was a member of the Stone Harbor Yacht Club and, more importantly, had use of his father's car. We spent most of our afternoons on the beach or offshore fishing or sailing. With the car, our evenings were spent with friends at nearby Jersey Shore resort towns: Avalon and Ocean City. The pay wasn't great, but we ate well and saved enough to have some spending money when we returned to college.

My brother, Dennis, began his senior year at Villanova when I returned as a sophomore. He was living on campus, having won a four-year full ROTC scholarship. He became a Navy ensign when he graduated, having committed to serve for three years as a condition of the scholarship.

The sophomore schedule seemed lighter than the year before. There were fewer long breaks between classes and most of my classwork was over by midafternoon. My grades were above average, so I felt like being more active in sports. I had been playing in intramural basketball competition. Villanova varsity basketball always attracted scholarship players; that door was closed. But the college tennis team was recruited from the college ranks. I had played regularly at Bar Harbor and was pleased to find that I made the team.

Eagles Mere

Having been delighted by my summer at Stone Harbor, I resisted the idea of being with my parents in Maine in 1951. Mom, through Mrs. Browning, introduced me to Mrs. Rhoda Morris Hutchison, a Philadelphia lady who needed a driver for the summer. She was a true blue blood, a descendant from three signers of the Declaration of Independence. She was just recovering from a bout with tuberculosis, and her doctor suggested she vacation in the mountains above 2,000 feet, which was the ragweed line recognized by allergy sufferers.

I visited Mrs. Hutchison at her penthouse apartment in a building across from the Barclay Hotel on Rittenhouse Square in midtown Philadelphia. I tried not to appear nervous. She was gracious and had a reassuring smile. A job was offered. She didn't want to put on airs, didn't want me dressed in livery. She suggested that I buy a dark suit and shirts, charging her account at Wanamaker's.

We were to spend the summer at Eagles Mere in the Allegheny Mountains above Williamsport, Pennsylvania. She owned a new Cadillac limousine with a sliding glass window separating the driver from the passengers. I didn't know anything about Eagle's Mere, but I was thrilled to be working for her.

Mrs. Hutchison would be accompanied by a lady companion, Anne Thatcher. Mrs. Thatcher was from a respected Philadelphia family; her husband had died, leaving her a modest estate.

They patiently waited until early June when I was ready to take off for the mountains. I received excellent directions from AAA and asked friends if they knew people in Eagles Mere. Tom Hayden, a Villanova classmate from Merion, Pennsylvania, told me to look up his friends Lou and Joe Haenn.

The drive to Eagles Mere was simple, northwest past Reading and Bloomsburg to 42 North. We were there in less than three hours. Our destination was the Lakeside Hotel. This was a 320-room, white painted cedar shingled resort structure. Mrs. Hutchison and Mrs. Thatcher shared the hotel's largest suite. I was assigned a room and bath overlooking the lake. The owner, Mr. Kirk, welcomed us in a gracious manner. The ladies were assigned a table in the dining room, and I was given one nearby. Both tables were served by the same waitress, Marilyn Fox, a freshman student from Duquesne University in Pittsburgh.

Each day I awaited instructions as to what I should do to earn my keep. After breakfast on the first day, I was asked to visit with my boss on the porch for a chat. I learned that they planned to stay close to the hotel and their need for the car would be limited. I realized that it was up to me to plan how to enjoy all this free time.

It must have raised eyebrows to see this out-of-town young man driving around town in a fancy new Cadillac limo. I spent afternoons at the beach and met several same age guys who enjoyed tennis and sailing. The Lakeside Hotel had a gameroom with ping-pong and pool tables. One evening in late June, I was playing pool with Hod Lippencot, the publisher's son, and Ted Wood, whose family owned Allan Wood Steel Co. Hod and Ted were a couple of Yale students. They were both excited about being ticketed to attend the Republican National Convention as Eisenhower supporters.

Our game was interrupted by a pageboy outfitted with a Phillip Morris-style pillbox hat. She called out, "Paging Mr. Craig. Paging Mr. Craig." I was informed that I had visitors in the main lobby.

I was surprised when I met Lou (Louise) Haenn, mentioned by Tom Hayden. I came out with the dumbest remark. "I thought that Tom wanted me to meet two guys, Lou and Joe."

Louise's friend, Nancy Hales, was charming and suggested we get together for a visit at her home the next evening. I was delighted to meet them, and little did I know it would have significant bearing on the rest of my life.

The next evening, Louise and I played bridge with Nancy and

her date. Soon after, Louise and I enjoyed swimming, tennis, and boating together.

Eagles Mere (EM) is a very small borough in Sullivan County, Pennsylvania. Eighty percent of the county is state-owned parkland. Eagles Mere Lake, only a mile in diameter, is in the center of the borough. It has been referred to as "the town time forgot." Lake access still is controlled by the Eagles Mere Association, which has about 350 summer residents, fee-paying family memberships. Year-round families have lake access without paying membership fees. The Association and conservation foundation own most of the surrounding forests.

On my first visit to EM, there were four large hotels, including the Lakeside. They're all gone now. Prior to 1948, only one road went up the 2,000-foot mountain. After the Bar Harbor fire, seven miles of new road were built to the town of Laporte. Both then and now, in addition to the beach, the Eagles Mere Golf Club was a center of social activity, with an 18-hole golf course, several tennis courts, and fine dining. Louise included me in club activities. She was from Merion, Pennsylvania, a Philadelphia suburb. Her family lived on a large property on Montgomery Avenue. She was one of eight children, and Joe was her older brother. They were two years apart. She had five younger sisters and a middle-of-the-pack brother, Bob. It was a bit unnerving to sit at a family dinner as one of 11, having grown up with two brothers, where one person spoke at a time. At Springwood, the Haenn summer cottage, conversations were going on around the table all the time. As the newcomer, I was fielding questions throughout the meal.

By mid-July, Mrs. Hutchison had become weary of the hotel and, feeling better, she decided she no longer needed to remain in the mountains. She and Mrs. Thatcher seemed especially spirited one morning after breakfast. They invited me to join them. Seated comfortably on the hotel porch, they regaled me with laughter, referring to tales they heard from Marilyn Fox. All the hotels were staffed with college students who frequently got together gabbing on one of the docks, at the activities center, or at the sweet shop. From time to time, I joined that crowd and was Marilyn's date.

Mrs. Hutchison said, "Bill, I know you're enjoying Eagles Mere; I hope it won't upset you if we arrange to spend August at Cape May on the Jersey Shore. We've talked with Marilyn, and not wanting to get you both upset, we've asked her to come along. She said if I agree it sounded like fun to her."

Having spent the previous summer at Stone Harbor and since Cape May was the next town down the coast, to me it was just more of a good thing. Not wanting to cause an embarrassment, without a minute's delay, I said, "Forget about me. I'm having a great summer, thanks to you. Let's go to Cape May, but I wouldn't want my parents to hear about taking Marilyn with us. I don't think it would be fair to Louise either."

Cape May

Driving from Eagles Mere to Cape May was the second time in a month that I had them in the back seat. We were booked to stay for the month of August at the Admiral Hotel, the tallest New Jersey coast building. It was, like the Greenbriar, used as a hospital and recovery center during World War II. It had just been redecorated and they did a super job. My ladies had an elaborate suite, and I had a lovely oceanside room on the 8th floor. Again I was assigned a separate table in the main dining room. I proceeded to resume life with other college-age kids, having a summer to remember. "What a job!"

I was only asked three times to take them out to dine at local restaurants. Twice we went to the Bay View, once for lunch and once for dinner. Both times I was asked to join them. The third lunch outing was to Henry's, famous for French cuisine. I let them out at the curb in front of the restaurant and joined them at their table. It was a fun meal. When we left the restaurant and got into the car, I couldn't find the keys in my pocket. I panicked, got flustered, and felt really stupid.

My unbelievable boss said, "Don't get upset. Just go into the restaurant and call a cab."

After the taxi picked them up and drove them back to the hotel, I arranged to have new keys made. While still in Cape May, I had a surprise visitor. Louise had arranged with a mutual friend, Eddie Walsh, to drive down from Philadelphia for the day. Ed was a high school buddy whose family had a summer place at Ocean City. We had a great visit with dinner at Bay View restaurant. Louise was glowing in her summer tan and was charming in the lighthearted way she engaged in conversation. When I waved goodbye, I thought how much fun it would be to date her back in Philadelphia.

Mrs. Hutchison asked me when I had to go back to Villanova. When I said it would be during the first week in September, she said, "We'll be sure to get you back in time." We checked out a week later.

When I returned home to Upper Darby, my mother and brother Jack were back from Bar Harbor. Brother Den was off to sea as a junior US Navy officer, fulfilling his ROTC obligation. My father and the family car were still in Maine. I mention the family car, for while neither my mother nor my younger brother Jack were drivers, I would be grounded except for the wonderful thoughtful Mrs. Rhoda Morris Hutchison. On our way back from Cape May to Philadelphia, she asked if I needed the car to go back to school. I explained that my dad and Mr. Browning would not be returning until October. I could hardly believe my luck when she said, "Well, Bill, I suppose your family garage will be empty. Just keep my car until your father returns from Maine. Otherwise, it's foolish to put it in storage in the city if you can use it."

Sometimes you could hug your boss.

I now could avoid taking the P&W for two months. However, I'm sure I was the only Villanova student who arrived daily in a limo carrying a brown bag containing a peanut butter sandwich and an apple.

I was surprised one evening when dating Louise, who was just back from Eagles Mere. We were parked in the limo next to her family garage and, reaching my right arm around her shoulder, I was shocked to find over the glass partition the set of car keys supposedly lost outside Henry's at Cape May. This is my secret, first time revealed.

It was in the summer of my sophomore year that I met Louise. She had just graduated from Mater Misericordia Academy. Her school shared a very large estate property with Waldron Academy, both operated by the Sisters of Mercy. The boys attended Waldron, and the Haenn sisters attended Mater Misericordia.

The schools were on Montgomery Avenue across from the family home in Merion, Pennsylvania. I dated Louise off and on throughout my junior year. She did not apply for college. She had a lifetime dream of becoming a nurse, but a foot condition prevented her from taking that career path.

We saw much more of each other during my senior year. You might say we were going steady. We attended ballgames, movies, parties, and dances. We went out together New Year's Eve and attended my formal senior prom.

Villanova College was an all male school. It was universal then for men and women to attend single sex high schools and colleges. Louise attended an all girls academy. Her mother graduated in 1911 from Trinity, a women's Catholic college in Washington, D. C. She also received a graduate degree from the Sorbonne in Paris. Dr. Haenn received his Doctor of Veterinary Medicine from the University of Pennsylvania. He never went into medical practice but joined his father in the lumber and construction supply business.

The Korean War

Every day throughout my college years, the news was about battles in Korea. The US entered the Korean War in 1950, only four years following the end of World War II. Americans felt invincible, the most powerful country in the world. I thought we would be in and out of this conflict in short order. Our initial response was half-hearted until our combined troops were pushed to the southernmost part of the peninsula. The US significantly increased forces, opening a new front by way of the Inchon invasion, driving the North Koreans all the way north to the Yellow River, at the Chinese border. The Chinese army joined North Korean forces, pushing our troops south. General MacArthur wanted to add more US forces and move across the Yellow River into China. President Truman relieved MacArthur of duty and the back and forth led to a battlefield stalemate, which brought about a ceasefire. The border between North and South Korea returned to the 38th parallel where it has remained for the past 64 years. The Korean War officially ended July 23, 1953.

In my senior year, it seemed certain I would be drafted upon graduation. I assumed it was most likely I would be inducted into the Army. I didn't mind responding to the call, but if possible I would rather be engaged in a military activity that would give me training useful in the future. Seeking information along those lines, I visited a recruitment office, sought out discharged veterans, and spoke with classmates who had service experience.

One of my accounting instructors told me that his service was a career plus for him. He suggested looking into making application for the Counter Intelligence Corps. The CIC had a regional office in the Philadelphia National Bank building in midtown Philadelphia. When I visited the office, I noticed that there was no one dressed in military uniform. I learned that to be trained as a CIC agent I would have to volunteer, serve at least three years, receive a Top Secret clearance, have a college degree, and pass the Officers Training School (OCS) test.

The drawback was spending a year longer in the service than if I were taken through the draft. Since the program required over a year of training, it made sense to be on call for three years of service. The suggestion was made to think about it. I filled out the application and decided to volunteer and enlist to become a CIC agent.

I knew the military future was soon and irrevocable, but I wondered what else might be out there. I was invited to a job interview with the accounting firm, Arthur Young, at their New York City Woolworth Building headquarters. They put me through some tests, but when they understood I was draft eligible, there seemed to be a question about reimbursement for travel and hotel expenses that I had been told not to worry about. After the test results came in, I was invited to return to a job following my discharge.

Planning to enter the service in July, I chose to spend the between time at Bar Harbor. Brother Jack and I enjoyed time together, and we were welcomed by the park service to our old jobs clearing trails at Acadia National Park. There could be no better way to shape up for basic training than climbing mountains and sawing logs as a daily routine.

Counter Intelligence Corps

In mid-July, I went by bus to Bangor, Maine, took an overnight train to New York, and another train to Philadelphia. Our Copley Road house was closed for the summer, but I was invited to stay overnight at the Haenn house. Dr. Haenn was there tending to business. He would only go to Eagles Mere for weekends.

The next day, Louise took me downtown to the Army induction center and waved me off when I boarded a train heading for Fort Meade, Maryland. It didn't take long after arriving at Fort Meade to realize that being a recruit was intimidation by design. There was little room for individuality. The first step of induction was to strip for medical inspection.

I have been medically inspected many times, but I was never instructed to wait standing naked in line for forty-five minutes. For the life of me I couldn't see why this medic took so long to do what in army lingo is a "short arm inspection." The final dehumanizing blow was the quickest part of the process — the GI haircut. A tough looking big guy with an electric razor stripped me of my crowning glory in less than a minute. Thank God, when he was finished, he didn't hold up a mirror to meet the new me. It was as if they found me outside the front door in a basket with no identification. There was a steady stream of paperwork to be filled out. I began to wonder if there was information in their file that I had already signed piles of forms designating that I had signed up for CIC. I was consoled by the thought that maybe that was a secret.

After three days, I was handed a couple of railroad and bus tickets and sent to Fort Dix, New Jersey, assigned to basic training for Heavy Infantry. Fort Dix is in south Jersey, where locally it's called the sand barrens, an excellent place to be marched around for miles. It's flat.

I was assigned to a barracks resembling some of the dormitories at Villanova. It made me glad to have been a commuter. The buildings at Villanova were described as BOQ— Basic Officers Quarters.

The one distinguishing characteristic about heavy infantry is the battle use of the mortar, which consists of a barrel tube and a baseplate. Put them together, drop an explosive device into the tube and, directed by a forward observer, it can be a very effective weapon. Its use goes back hundreds of years; however, it's heavy lifting. I found out firsthand when marching 15 to 20 miles carrying either the baseplate at 40 pounds or a barrel of similar weight.

The quartermaster at Fort Dix lined us up on the first day to receive our uniforms. At the time, I weighed 150 pounds and was six feet tall. My mother referred to me as a string bean. The assigned uniforms seemed to fit okay, and the boots were great for hiking for miles. But carrying heavy equipment was a ticket for blistered feet.

My only concern about the issued clothing was the boxer shorts. I had an extremely narrow waist and was issued the smallest size, but even when tying the tabs as tight as possible my shorts still slid down. Fortunately, inspection never called for dropping your drawers. I solved the problem by wearing shorts from home.

Thank God I became fit when working for the National Park Service. Most of basic training was dedicated to shaping up with physical exercise. Having spent a month climbing up and down mountains, I was in great shape. One of the early events in basic training was taking OCS qualifying tests. I knew from the beginning that failing to qualify would leave me in the infantry.

In a roomful of would-be's I sat with butterflies in my stomach, hoping I wouldn't panic under the pressure. There were four sections and, while I thought I did well, time ran out with a few essay questions yet to be answered. Out of hundreds in the training unit, there were fewer than 30 who took the test. A week later, they called out alphabetically the names of those who passed. I held my breath until they announced my name.

All I needed now was a Top Secret clearance. I knew they were on the job when I got word from my father that CIC agents from the Bangor office visited Pointe d'Acadie to speak with Mrs. Browning. I had no idea how many lifetime contacts would be interviewed; nor did I care.

I grudgingly accepted my turn at KP (washing pots and pans) without complaint. Every two weeks, I received a weekend pass. The weekend I wanted to return to Philadelphia was in October. I was scheduled to be my brother Den's best man. He was a lieutenant in the Navy and was getting married to Jane Keating, a girl he dated throughout his college years.

She graduated from Immaculata, a Catholic women's college. She lived with her parents, about five miles from Copley Road in Lansdowne, Pennsylvania.

Unfortunately, I got caught with KP and was unable to get a bus to Philadelphia to be on time for the wedding or the reception. Dad stood in for me. After the married couple headed off for their honeymoon, I caught up with both families, still celebrating at Jane's parents' home. My parents were there and, much to my delight, so was Louise.

In early November, orders came through sending me to Fort Holabird in Baltimore, the CIC headquarters. I would be there for more than a year. Fort Holabird is on the bay side of Baltimore in the neighborhood known as Dundalk. I was right to assume that the training and experience would be carried forward to my business and social career. There were lessons on conducting interviews and interrogations, recognizing tone of voice, facial expression, eye contact and posture, how to question, and how to listen.

Most of the agent reports were stamped at least "confidential." The reports needed to be typed. In the 1950s, students were not typing. Business people dictated to secretaries, CIC agents typed their reports, and they were expected to phrase and spell correctly. Typing was slow for me. Having been a newspaper reporter and editor, composition was not a problem. Interrogation and surveillance required special skills and often required teamwork.

Actors were brought in to practice interrogation. Since a suspected crime scene required pictures, the classified photo film couldn't be developed commercially; therefore, we were trained and supplied with developing equipment, cameras, projectors, and enlargement equipment. There were also courses in lock picking and the installation of surreptitious listening devices.

Some of the special agent's time is spent performing investigations required for security clearance. Before my training at Fort Holabird was completed, I was issued a badge and shoulder holster with a 28-caliber snub-nosed pistol.

Our group was given individual assignments. My assignment was San Antonio, Texas, where I conducted security clearance interviews out of a downtown office. Shortly thereafter I was reassigned to the 4th Armored Division at Fort Hood, Killeen, Texas. The CIC unit at Fort Hood had three agents and two administrative staff. Shortly after arrival, a trunk came from Fort

Holabird containing equipment, including cameras, developing, and printing devices.

Fort Hood is the home of the 3rd Armored Corps made up of three divisions. There's a need for a lot of room for tank training and maneuvering. The base is 78 miles across and is populated by over 40,000 soldiers. We were assigned to a building that served as both offices and living quarters. The five team members each had separate rooms with baths. The three special agents were issued officer uniforms without rank insignia, and we were given use of the Officers Club.

Receiving Fort Hood tennis trophy from Major General Gates.

In the 1950s, "Jim Crow" laws were prevalent throughout the southern states. Texas was no exception. African Americans were referred to as Negroes, and public facilities were segregated. Public drinking fountains were labeled "Black" or "White." This was also true about public bathrooms, taxi service, hotels, motels, restaurants, and "Back of the Bus" treatment. This wasn't to get national attention until Martin Luther King challenged these practices in the mid-'60s.

In 1953–54, Senator Joseph McCarthy shook up the nation with his accusations that our government was loaded with communist and pinko sympathizers. He especially accused the State Department and the military by using shoddy evidence and often no evidence. He upset the country with televised threats and accusations during several open sessions of the US Senate. The US Army brass steamed about these accusations and directed the CIC to be more alert to any possible communist activity.

The question was: "Who and in what circumstances could a person in the military be approached or recruited and exploited by the Communists?" It was clear to me and obvious to headquarters that having thousands of black officers and enlisted men from northern states serving in "Jim Crow" country, they might be targeted. With an associate, we went about seeking information sources in cities near the Fort Hood area: Waco, Temple, Killeen, Gatesville, and Austin.

The plan was to seek out trusted black officers and enlisted men who frequented these towns on weekends. We looked for help in identifying good-spirited proprietors who owned services restricted to colored people (bars, cafés, restaurants, hotels, and taxis). We needed introductions and help was granted. We avoided making contact but counted on getting feedback from trusted supporters of the program.

We made direct contact in one instance with a master sergeant, who won support from the head of a black-owned cab company in Austin. The owner invited us to come and meet his family in Austin. He owned 30 cabs and only served colored people. He was a veteran, as were some of his drivers who liked to help in any way they could. I was informed that a Sunday meeting would be scheduled. The meeting had to end by 8 o'clock because it was unlawful for whites to be in that neighborhood after 7:30 pm. It was understood that our only interest was in hateful threats to authorities and pronounced commitments to un-American activities with Communist sympathizers. As far as I know, there never was any feedback. In spite of the unfair treatment of black GI's serving in the South, there were no signs of disloyalty.

POWs Seeking Preferred Treatment

The worst assignment I received had to do with US soldiers held as prisoners of war by Chinese troops in Korea. The POW camps were located just below the Yellow River in Korea. Several GI prisoners sought preferred treatment by cooperating with their captors at the expense of fellow prisoners, a court martial offense. Army regulations direct that enemy held soldiers restrict their response to interrogation with name, rank, and serial number. There were 28 men accused of cooperating; they remained in North Korea for as long as seven years, afraid of reprisals if they came home. Such cooperation often led to severe punishment of fellow inmates: beatings, solitary confinement, starvation, and other forms of torture. Partnered with another special agent, we were given a list of suspects and victims, some on active duty and some honorably discharged.

These men spent time in those POW camps where those transgressions occurred. We proceeded to collect depositions, interviewing men still on active duty and discharged veterans living in the area between Dallas and Austin. It was not an easy assignment. Most men we talked to were suspicious as to whether they were about to receive compassion or accusation, a pat on the back or prosecution. I'm glad that wasn't my call.

Serving my time in the military was not my idea of a career objective. It was a commitment I couldn't dodge. I think I made the most of it. But I don't want to close this chapter, one could call time in Texas with the Army, without sharing the best unbelievable experience I witnessed while living in the Lone Star State.

The town closest to Killeen is Lampasas, about 15 miles west. Locals whom I knew and respected told me that I had the good fortune to be in the area to witness the election campaign speeches at the Lampasas courthouse, especially one speaker. "What could possibly be interesting about a campaign speech?"

With a slap at his hip and a smile, my friend said, "The coroner is up for reelection. Roy Taylor, the incumbent, is scheduled to speak. He has been coroner for 40 years and reelected to the office every four years."

I said, "10 times? What's so strange about that?"

"Every four years he gives the same speech."

With a six-pack in the back seat, we drove to Lampasas, which is in Bell County, Texas. The crowd at the courthouse on the center square was packed, all awaiting Coroner Taylor. The 72-year old coroner stepped to the mic at center stage, wearing an empty holster strapped to his belt, waved his wide-brimmed hat, and thanked the crowd for coming.

"Ladies and gentlemen, thanks for your support. Again I'm asking for your vote. Back in 1906 I was a rough rider in Cuba. The Spaniards had sunk our ship, and we wanted to give them a lesson. Side by side with Theodore Roosevelt we rode up San Jaun Hill shooting right and left at them, and when we got to the top, we knew we had the best of them and they surrendered. Teddy looked at me and said, 'Roy, one day one of us may be elected President of the United States.' I replied, 'Teddy, I don't want to be President of the United States, I only hope to be coroner of Bell County, Texas.'"

For the 10th time in 40 years, the crowd went wild.

Don't mess with Texas. It's special; I'm glad I spent two years on duty there.

Honorably Discharged

In 1955, anticipating returning home to Philadelphia, I used my new typing skills to prepare 40 letters requesting job interviews. I got the names and addresses from the Philadelphia Chamber of Commerce executive directory. I included inquiries addressed to the Wharton graduate school at the University of Pennsylvania and the Harvard MBA program.

I was invited to visit both Harvard and Penn, which I did. My application could not be accepted for classes starting in September, but I was encouraged to enter both MBA programs beginning in February.

The response was encouraging, and when I got back to my parents' home in Upper Darby I had invitations to follow up with interviews at 30 companies. I'm glad I had the time and ability to type all those letters. Service in the Army was beginning to pay off.

Monday through Friday, for about a month, time was spent making appointments and seeing senior people at most of the large companies headquartered in the Philadelphia area. I accepted an offer to take a job with the Philadelphia Electric Co. in the statistical department. The executive offices were located at Center City, 10th and Chestnut Streets. It was the beginning of my business career.

It was also time to get my social life back on track. While in the service, I welcomed letters and cards from Louise every week. There wasn't a need for much catch-up and we saw each other at least once a week for the next two years. On Christmas Eve, 1957, we became engaged and were married May 10, 1958. We bought a house in Lower Merion three months before our marriage and had it fully furnished by the time we said our vows.

Engagement picture - Christmas week 1957.

Louise had her nursing career aspirations evaporate when it was realized that being on her feet all day wasn't for her. She had been born with a club left foot and, while she had several corrective operations and there was no limp, it was exhausting to be running around all day. Louise took office training courses and went to work as a legal assistant with Barnes and Shorts, a law firm that specialized in the trucking industry. We bought a Studebaker convertible, the kind with a bullet nose-styled front. It was white with red interior trim. Our office jobs were located near each other so we shared the commute in our fancy car.

While I felt smart to skip waiting half a year to undertake an MBA program at Harvard or Penn, I still recognized the value of the degree and was pleased to sign up for the MBA program at Drexel University. It offered classes at night, four days a week, for three years. Classes were from 4 pm to 7 pm. My work hours were 8 am to 4 pm, but Philadelphia Electric encouraged me to begin the program and arranged for me to cut office time on school days by half an hour, 8 to 3:30. I was informed by the VP of Finance that I was part of their executive training program.

Over the next three years, I was shifted from the statistical department to the tax department and to the accounting policy department. The mid-1950s was the era during which IBM had developed mainframe computers, which companies like PECo with millions of customers used to revolutionize the back office. I was trained to program and find applications throughout the company. I created charts and graphs for rate case filings and annual reports. Returned proxy cards regarding the annual meeting were directed to my desk for written response and for the President's signature. While continuing a membership in the American Statistical Society, I was asked to forecast industrial production for Delaware Valley by the Philadelphia Federal Reserve Office. PECo maintained monthly records of delivered power by class: industrial, commercial, and residential. Charting those industrial numbers gave the Fed the reliable forecast they were looking for.

With the addition of Drexel time, the workday routine was stretched to 10 hours, from 8 am to 7 pm, not counting commuting time. The commute was now switched to the train. I would walk from the office to a Philadelphia suburban station and take the Paoli local, which stopped at 30th Street Pennsylvania railroad station near Drexel. After classes I retunred on the local, which serves the Philadelphia main line.

Fortunately, PECo had a company-owned country club, near our home, with an 18-hole golf course and several tennis courts. The club was freely available to employees, and I frequently took advantage of the perks. Louise no longer needed to run in and out of town. She was too busy having babies. Within three years, we had two sons: Bill, Jr. and Matt.

Advanced by Writing

Completing my MBA required a written thesis. Luckily I selected a topic that was of great concern to public utilities and to commercial and investment banks that raised capital for the rapidly expanding industry. My thesis title was, "The Impact of Liberalized Depreciation on Public Utility Rate Making." Recent changes in the IRS Tax Code and accepted accounting allowed corporations to choose between different kinds of depreciation.

Utility rates are based on a fair return on invested capital dedicated to public use. Most utility company investment is in equipment for generation, transmission, and distribution. These capital-intensive projects normally have a useful life of 30 years on average! The ideal financing was to issue bonds with matching maturities and depreciation write-downs on a similar straight line schedule of 30-years.

When depreciation is accelerated for tax purposes, earnings are improved. The issue is who benefits: the rate paying customer or shareholders. If at the same time straight line depreciation is used for book accounting, the asset value reduces more slowly and extends the bondable equipment life used for collateral.

Putting on my statistician's hat, I designed a questionnaire on the subject and mailed it to every state and federal regulatory agency overseeing utilities. Records show that most academic surveys sent to regulators are discarded. About 70% of the information solicitations I mailed were answered, usually with a request to return a copy of my summary and recommendations.

The resulting thesis was published in the *Public Utilities Fortnightly*, a biweekly widely circulated magazine in the utility and financial industries. The most flattering comments came from the VP of Finance at PECo. He said, "I'm glad we gave you the half hour off each day for you to take night classes."

Frequently I read articles in the *Public Utilities Fortnightly* written by John Childs, who headed the Utility Department at Irving Trust Company, located at One Wall Street in New York City. We corresponded about published articles he had written. His office made more utility construction loans than any other Wall Street bank. Our communication led to an invitation to join Irving Trust.

Since I had commuted on public transportation to high school, to college, to graduate school, and to my Philadelphia office, I wasn't fazed with the challenge to commute from suburban Philadelphia to New York City and did so for the first six months on the new job. On Monday at 6 am, Louise would drop me off at 30th Street station for a Pennsylvania railroad ride to Newark, New Jersey, and there I'd switch to a subway through Hoboken to Manhattan. This routine got me to One Wall Street by 9 am.

I was 30 years old in 1961 and confident that if everything worked out, I'd be moving my family to the New York City area. I hoped the commute from Philadelphia would be temporary. The commute became routine. On Mondays and Wednesdays, I stayed overnight at the Downtown Athletic Club. On Tuesday evenings I went back to Philadelphia, returning to New York on

Wednesday. On Thursday I returned to Philadelphia, and on Friday I went both ways. The Downtown Athletic Club was great, with squash courts, fitness center, swimming pool, and two fine restaurants. It was famous as a sports club, since it annually awarded the Heisman Trophy. The Club was only three blocks from Wall Street. While staying there two nights a week, I met several young men in similar circumstances, allowing me to enjoy friendly company at dinner.

The Haenn Family

I was encouraged by my assignments and my acceptance into the bank.

The decision to move to New York came after a day when I left 30th Street station at 6 am in a January blizzard, arriving at 6 pm in Newark. It was obviously time to make our move.

Without a word of complaint, Louise was ready, willing, and able to pack up and move to the New York area. Our aim was to buy a home in New Jersey within a short commuting distance to downtown New York City, where we would have less than a two-hour drive back to Philadelphia.

It would have been harsh to expect Louise to forgo her beneficial social ties and her recognition as a member of such a remarkable and respected family. Her mother's grandfather was the founder of the Union News Company in Cincinnati, Ohio, which spread across the country selling newspapers, magazines, cigarettes, candy, etc. from stands in most railroad stations. She grew up in Germantown, north of Philadelphia.

Her maiden name was Felin. Her father owned the Felin meat packing company with three slaughterhouses and 52 butcher shops in Pennsylvania, New Jersey, and Delaware. Both parents died young, and she was an heiress in her 20s when she became chairman of the board. The war years were a strain for butcher shops, and post-war years were worse. Food store chains expanded one-stop shopping, putting butchers and bakers out of business. Felin Meat Packing Co. was sold to Morell in Chicago. Louise's father never practiced veterinary medicine after receiving his doctorate at Penn in 1917. He was commissioned to serve as an officer in the cavalry, but at the same time was commissioned into the Quartermaster Corps. His assignment was to oversee the loading of ships serving the WWI war effort at the ports of New York, Philadelphia, and Baltimore. His father and grandfather owned Haenn Lumber Co. and Haenn Ship Sealing Co., with operations in Philadelphia, New Jersey, and Baltimore. Haenn Ship Sealing Co. had dozens of men employed at these ports, securing cargo with wood from Haenn lumber mills. One of the mills was located on land where the Delaware and Schuylkill Rivers meet. Dr. Haenn's father sold part of that land on which the Atlantic Refinery was built.

During World War II, Haenn Lumber was approved by the government to crate Signal Corps equipment for overseas shipment. They had contracts with GE, Philco, RCA, and other companies.

Dr. Haenn and I had a very fond relationship. During the summer months, we traveled to and from Eagles Mere together on weekends, frequently stopping for dinner.

Dr. and Mrs. Haenn on a Holland America Line cruise ship
on the way to Europe.

Moving to New York

When the decision was made to buy a house in North Jersey,
Dr. Haenn joined Louise and me in searching neighborhoods
for the right place. The search was narrowed down to Summit,
Chatham, and Short Hills. The more often we visited the area,
the more excited we became about the move.

In the spring of 1962, we sold our suburban Philadelphia house for $20,000 and moved into the Short Hills house we bought for $21,500. It was an ideal location within walking distance to church and parochial school, and was only four blocks from the commuter rail line, Erie & Lackawanna, that had express service to Hoboken.

The job in the Utility Department at Irving Trust was better than expected. I was away from home one week a month selling construction loans to power companies and gas pipelines in need of capital for expansion. These companies were overseen by state and federal regulation. Every state had a separate regulatory commission. Only one company per city could install poles for overhead wires or dig up roads for gas.

Since there was rarely more than one utility in a city, my trips made me into a frequent flyer. It was not uncommon to make a week's trip from New York to Chicago, to St. Louis, to Denver, to Dallas, to Houston, and back to New York.

Being identified with John Childs was a real plus. The department had only two VP assistants to Childs when I arrived as his third assistant. I received an AVP title after my first year.

John Childs was brilliant and one of the most respected authorities on the subject of "cost of capital." He received his BS in mathematics from Trinity College, an MBA from Harvard, and a law degree from Columbia. Identifying with Childs was a real door opener. I assisted him in writing a textbook, *Long Term Financing*, published by Prentiss Hall, and participated as an instructor at week-long seminars for senior utility executives and regulators.

These seminars included an introduction to Wall Street with visits to the floor of the stock exchange to learn how a specialist operates, to the rating agencies, to security analyst meetings, and to Salomon Brothers regarding bond bidding. Sessions included speakers from First Boston and Goldman Sachs regarding trading, arbitrage, valuation of rights during stock offerings, and the calculation of cost of capital for rate regulation. Included in these programs were often visits with Henry Kaufman at Salomon, Sidney Weinberg at Goldman Sachs, and Alan Greenspan at NYU.

The Utility Department seminars were so successful there was hope that such programs could provide similar benefit to national division officers soliciting business from out-of-town commercial corporations. It was decided to expand the seminar programs to include financial executives from non-utilities. One of the first groups included my brother, Dennis, who was treasurer at Armstrong Cork Co. in Lancaster, Pennsylvania.

Brother Dennis (left) with Bill visiting the
New York Federal Reserve gold vault.

With seminar alumni in just about every utility company throughout the United States, there was never a cold call on the road. No other Wall Street bank had that advantage. Our unit put together multi-million-dollar financings. When top corporate officials came to town for an analyst meeting or financing closing, it was an opportunity to entertain them, often with their wives at dinner and the theater. It would often include a lunch at the bank hosted by Irving's chairman or president with me attending. Most junior officers never have such opportunities to form a good relationship with the top brass.

Remembering the leg up I got from getting published, I went back to writing articles for financial publications. Selecting narrow subjects made me appear to be an expert on some current topics. The hope was that recognition might help move me along.

WRITING REWARDS

A good example is now part of history. In the mid-1960s, interest on most bonds was serviced by clipped coupons. Historically, the bond owner or the bond owner's custodian would quarterly or semi-annually clip a coupon attached to the bond face and deposit it through the banking system for payment. How could such a system continue in this computer age?

I had discussions with investment banks that had significant bond underwriting business, had long meetings with agencies involved with clearing coupon deposits, and had meetings with officers at the New York Federal Reserve. *Investment Dealer's Digest* published my study in an article titled, "The Growing Acceptance of Registered Bonds." Writing published articles added credibility, and the notice offered career advantages.

Recognition coming from published articles, even on relatively narrow subjects, expands career opportunities. Shortly after the release of the bond coupon article, I was invited to have lunch at Salomon Brothers with Billy Salomon, John Gutfreund, and Henry Kaufman. Their company was a major underwriter of utility bonds. Their success resulted from low bids at auctioned bond offerings, not through relationships. They were of the opinion that my utility company contacts might strengthen their aim to attract negotiated underwritings.

At that time, Louise and I had added four more to our Short Hills family, with three sons and three daughters in six years. We had just moved into a larger house and, while the mortgage was manageable, I felt it was no time to bet that I was up to fulfilling

Salomon's desires, in spite of the big numbers they offered. Bill Simon had just left the firm to become Secretary of the Treasury. The investment bank was on a roll. This was only four years after joining Irving, where I felt I had a secure future.

Meanwhile the president of Prudential Insurance Co. contacted Bill Peterson, president of Irving Trust, and out of courtesy and as a major account of the bank, he said he would like to talk to me about possibly joining Prudential. Complimented by the interest, I was off to Newark the following week. The Prudential, at that time, was only invested in bonds, holding not a single equity share. In the mid-'60s, it was common to match actuarial obligations to long-term investment maturities. At that time, AT&T's pension fund held no stocks.

Equities, which had been flat for ages, began showing some signs of upward movement. The Prudential felt it was time to include a moderate amount of common stock in their investment accounts and believed the place to begin was in bank and utility equities. They were looking for someone to make such investments. The job offer was made, and the flattery enjoyed; I knew where I stood with Irving Trust, so why take the risk that the stock market would rise to please Prudential's hopes? Six kids under six spells risk aversion. The Prudential was disappointed, but Bill Peterson was all smiles when I told him I wanted to stay with Irving. He announced that he wanted me to break away from being a specialist and move through several departments to become a fully trained banker. Soon I was elected a vice president and moved to loan administration, which functions as the final step for loan approval.

Any loan over $2 million passed through Loan Administration. Most approvals were for credit lines for large long-established relationships, and they were sound risks. Whenever there was an elevated risk, it called for a conference, including the originating officer, the division head, and the senior loan administration officer, who was an executive vice president. This was a learning experience requiring a thorough review of the file and careful attention to the back and forth concerning the details. I learned something about credit judgment: usually after asking 20 questions one can be 95 percent sure; asking another 10 questions may make the certainty 96 percent. But passing the approval judgment to a more senior officer was a roadblock for increased loan authority. The lending business demands a yes or no.

Loan administration was an exercise every bit as instructive as an MBA case study, with the added element of real money. After involvement with the approval process, I was shifted to the collection department. You'd think the first question asked of a borrower would be, "How am I going to get my money back?" Some of the loans that landed in collection begged the question.

The biggest frustrations were foreclosures and bankruptcies. It's a whole different world involving personalities and relationships between judges and lawyers on both sides. It's not a business for the impatient. I was brought in as a member of the credit committee for the Penn Central bankruptcy. Paul Volcker was a member of the six-man committee. He represented Citibank. All I remember about that fiasco is that everyone lost but the lawyers. For them, it was a bonanza.

The Penn Central bankruptcy was a heavy shock to Wall Street. In hindsight, you could see it coming.

Just about every Sunday throughout the winter months, from 1 pm to 3 pm, I played tennis on clay courts inside a lofted greenhouse with glass walls, full of gorgeous plants and fountains. It was on the Frelinghuysen estate in Madison, New Jersey. The foursome included Fred Kirby, Gerry McGinley, Bob Coen, and me.

Fred's father, Alan Kirby, had, through Allegheny Corp, acquired control of the New York Central Railroad. Fred's father died and Fred took over the railroad. He was agreeable to the merger with the Pennsylvania Railroad; the Pennsylvania, being larger, assumed the management. Fred was on the combined board and brought along three other New York central directors. One Sunday, to my surprise, he confided that he was resigning from the Penn Central board. He stated that the company management was not giving board members requested information, and he believed that a director's responsibility could only be effective if he carried in his pocket a resignation letter to every board meeting. Such a resignation was sure to bring attention from the financial press and the SEC.

"Bill, this is what I would like you to do. I want the stock controlled by the family transferred to a trust account at your bank with instructions to sell all of it after I quit the board and two quarterly reports are released to shareholders. I wouldn't want to be accused of trading on inside information." The Penn Central stock was selling in the $50 per share range. He was sold out per instructions six months later at $6 per share. His original valuation exceeded $100 million. He never once discussed it or suggested a change in instructions, with me or anyone at the bank. Irving Trust had a significant Penn Central loan outstanding. I would have been a hero if I had shared Fred's warning with the bank's senior management, but it would have been disclosing inside information.

Loan Collection

If you know what is needed to collect a bad loan, it follows that you should know how to analyze and document a good one.

It was decided that I should return to the loan production and account management side of the business. My next assignment was to the East Central District: Pennsylvania, Maryland, Washington, D.C., and West Virginia. A troubled credit situation headed by Irving Trust was Wheeling Steel, headquartered in Wheeling, West Virginia, with a controlling investor, Norton Simon. Simon was a West Coast investor who was famous in the canning business. His chief financial advisor was Gus Levy, Senior Managing Partner at Goldman Sachs. Wheeling Steel was over leveraged and had serious production problems. A new mill was poorly designed and the company lost control of inventory. Ingots were stacked without content codes; revenue fell short of debt payment requirements. It seemed to me that Wheeling's survival called for more capital and new management.

At a meeting with Jim Hughes at Mellon Bank in Pittsburgh, a participant in the credit, it was arranged to have lunch at the Duquesne Club with Henry Hillman, a significant investor in Pittsburgh Coke and Chemical Co, and Pittsburgh Steel Co. Mr. Hillman cut the meeting short in order to attend a board committee meeting at Pittsburgh National Bank but suggested we walk over together. Along the way, he encouraged me to follow up with the possibility of a merger.

Back in New York the following week, I met with Gus Levy at Goldman Sachs, the Wall Street investment bank for Norton Simon. I told him about the Hillman solution and got a cold, "It's not going to happen." Gus said that he happened to meet George Murphy, Irving's chairman, at a weekend social event and they agreed to extend the credit, allowing Wheeling Steel to remain independent.

I guess Levy had no idea how open relationships were at Irving, but within a half hour I was sitting in George Murphy's office where he confirmed that he had never spoken to Levy. The Wheeling Steel–Pittsburgh Steel deal was done and Irving was paid.

MOVING UP AT IRVING

My next assignment was to head the New England District of the National Division. As manager of the New England District, I couldn't believe I was being paid to go to Connecticut, Massachusetts, Rhode Island, New Hampshire, and Maine. Boston was the hub, but it was like a vacation to visit Maine. My fondest memories are associated with anticipation of the train trip from Philadelphia to Bar Harbor, often referred to as Philadelphia on the rocks. Every Sunday there was a Bar Harbor express train leaving Philadelphia 30th Street station at noon. All aboard were in assigned compartments with Sunday newspapers, Monopoly board game, cards, and Lego games; dinner in the dining car; beds made up during our meal; back to the compartments with shades drawn; ding, ding, ding at town crossings; and disembark at Ellsworth. Monday morning, Dad was waiting at the station.

While heading the New England District, I received a call from Wally Haselton, chairman of Depositors Trust Company in Augusta, Maine, an Irving correspondent. He related a concern expressed by Governor Curtis about the financial condition of one of the state's largest employers, Bates Manufacturing Corp. The company had 4,000 employees at three textile mills located in Augusta and Lewiston. He noted that a solution for the company's problems exceeded his capital limits. He identified the controlling stockholders as David Finkelstein, Chairman, Arnold Ginsberg, President, and Walter Jeffords, an investor Director. All were New York City residents.

A visit to the plants disclosed significant problems, such as the introduction of polyester fibers to what were traditional cotton mills; Bates' bedspreads suffered from an unacceptable level of seconds. They were unable to sell product at full price. These old mills with high humidity were not air conditioned, and the blended cotton could not produce a high standard product. Production was running at a 30 percent seconds rate. The polyester, an oil-based product, was being produced at a company-owned plant in Rocky Mount, North Carolina. The Maine governor was fearful that the entire manufacturing might be shifted to air-conditioned plants in North Carolina.

At my suggestion, the company engaged Arthur D. Little to see if a technical solution might be found. I discussed with Wachovia Bank in Winston-Salem, North Carolina, the possibility of putting together a bank credit secured by receivables and inventory. Arthur D. Little recommended production modifications, which would reduce seconds to less than 10 percent; but Bates was still short of adequate collateral. Much to my surprise, I discovered that Bates owned 50 percent of Virginia Iron Coal and Coke (VICC) located in Pulaski, Virginia. It came on their books through the purchase of a textile machine company. The Bates management had no idea what the unrelated business was worth, but it paid a steady dividend. I observed that the coal mining properties abutted properties mined and owned by the Pittston Coal Company. Realizing that my friend Fred Kirby was a Pittston director, I asked him to introduce me to senior Pittston management to see what they thought these properties might be worth.

Arrangements were made for me to meet with the Pittston chairman, J. P. Routh, and President Nick Comecia. I learned that VICC owned large acreage with quality reserves. The property was being mined primarily by many small nonunion contractors paying royalty fees to VICC. Pittston had no interest in VICC under existing conditions. However, they thought if a complete takeover ever came on the market, it might be worth $15 million. It was determined that the remaining 50 percent of VICC stock could be purchased for $2 million. A loan for that amount was made to Bates, and the stock of VICC, when added to other collateral, allowed Irving Trust and Depositors Trust to pump in the money needed to keep most of Bates in Maine. Wally Haselton became a fishing buddy for life.

Dad and Mom

In June 1965, I was attending a New Jersey Bankers' Association annual convention in Atlantic City, staying at the Hadden Hall Hotel on the Boardwalk. Returning to my room after attending a dinner followed by dull speeches, I had a call waiting. It was from my brother Jack reporting that my dad had suffered a heart attack and was at Fitzgerald Mercy Hospital in Darby, Pennsylvania. The next morning I drove to the hospital. Dad was 68 and had been burdened with heart problems for several months. He died the following November.

Mother came to stay with us at Short Hills in December, and after Christmas she was invited to stay for awhile with my brother Dennis, who had a lovely Georgian-style home on Broad Street in Lititz, Pennsylvania. Next door was a rented house that Mom later moved to shortly after my father's death. Brother Dennis had only one employer since his naval service. His entire career was with Armstrong Cork Co., headquartered in Lancaster, Pennsylvania. He worked his way up from credit manager, treasurer, vice president, and director.

Taking Mom from Short Hills to Lititz was an unforgettable

adventure. Louise joined us; Den and Jane invited us to stay overnight. The big mistake was choosing to take a low-slung car when the forecast was snow. It was a Pontiac LeMans, robin's egg blue, white-walled convertible. It was the week between Christmas and New Year's. The trip started at about 6 pm, a time when it was dark and beginning to snow. We went south on the New Jersey Turnpike to the Pennsylvania Turnpike, exiting at Ephrata. We were in Amish country with town names such as Paradise, Intercourse, and Blueballs. The country road wound through farmland, past only a few lighted houses. Amish people declined the use of electricity. The snowstorm was coming from the west, and after four hours of accumulated drifts on less traveled country roads, we came to a dip in the road and were facing a snowdrift that had to be four feet high. The front of the car dug in, and even the headlights were buried. Prayer was never more tested than at that moment. We couldn't see a light in any direction. You might think that blowing your car horn would only be more stupid than driving on a country road at night in a snowstorm. No, it was brilliant. Coming through the snow fence on the hill above the road were five farmers wearing shoulder-strapped overalls and carrying shovels. They were like the lifesavers who came to the beaches in storms to help pull shipwreck survivors out of the surf.

These farmers were alert about the risk people faced knowing how snow mounds up in this swale. The men calmly shoveled us clear, shoving the car around until it faced the way we came.

With our prayers answered, I got out of the car, pulled out my wallet and offered a cash reward. The men refused the money. I then handed over my business card and said, "Should a local charity need a gift for support, write to me."

About two weeks later, I received a letter asking for a donation for the local Volunteer Fire Department. I forwarded the letter to my mother. She responded with a real deflater. "Billy, when will you be on your own? Enclosed is a check for $800. Buy yourself some snow tires."

I deposited her check and sent $1,000 to the charity.

Soon after, I learned that Mrs. Browning informed my mother that she would be receiving Dad's salary for the rest of her life.

Leveraged Buyout

In early September 1969, George Murphy, Irving's chairman, called and asked me to join him for lunch later that week. He introduced me to the chairman of Paine Webber, Nelson Darling, Win Short, chairman of Knapp-Kingsize Corp., and David Place, partner of the Boston law firm of Gaston, Snow, Ely, and Bartlett. Knapp-Kingsize was a Brockton, Massachusetts, shoe and clothing company owned by NYU. George Murphy was chairman of NYU and Nelson Darling was another trustee of the University. They explained that several years ago NYU was gifted ownership of Knapp-Kingsize and Mueller's Macaroni Co. The New York State Attorney General questioned how a not-for-profit university, a tax-exempt organization, could own for-profit companies.

There was also a legal question about undistributed earnings. NYU decided to sell both companies. They had a buyer for Muller Macaroni, but they were unsure about Knapp-Kingsize. Win Short was hoping that a management leveraged buyout could be arranged. David Place was his lawyer. At that time, there was little involvement by investment banks in such transactions. I was asked to see if financing could be arranged. I was instructed that if bank credit was needed it would be a small piece, and it would only fit if another money center bank participated with Irving. We needed to avoid any conflict suspicion due to Mr. Murphy's dual roles. I was given a bundle of financial documents and was advised that NYU would not accept less than $20 million. Win Short mentioned that management would stretch to provide $2 million equity. Mr. Murphy stressed the importance of speedy action.

Normally I would have saluted and said something like, "I'll get right on it," except there was a previous commitment. Most bank loan officers would die for a chance to be singled out by the Chairman of the Board and CEO to find a solution to so personal a need. But very few young bankers had seven children at home. Yes, Louise and I were blessed with the April 1967 arrival of our seventh child, Margie. Mr. Murphy was fond of Louise, so hastily I mentioned that we had planned for a trip to Hawaii next week for the ABA annual meeting and a week of vacation. I could tell that Mr. Murphy felt awkward, knowing that he wanted the others at the table to realize he had conveyed the importance of the assigned mission. I said that I would start immediately to put together a plan and take action as soon as possible. I noted that Louise needed a vacation and she had put together over 100 peanut and jelly sandwiches, then stuffed them in the freezer, expecting the maid to prepare school lunches in our absence.

Mr. Murphy gave a thoughtful expression, smiled, and simply said, "Get your team to lay the groundwork and pick it up as soon as you get back."

Twenty million dollars was a stretch for Knapp-Kingsize. Knapp shoe was vulnerable to possible sudden revenue variations since 45 percent of the company's sales went to Sears. Their big product was steel-toed leather workboots. The product was fine, production management was excellent, but economic swings made cash flow vulnerable. Historically profitable performance was not dependable.

Kingsize, with a few outlet stores in New England, was primarily a catalog company for large men's clothing. The styles were good and orders were steady.

The timing for this deal was ahead of the buyout era that captivated Wall Street 10 years later.

Fortunately the company had no long-term debt. The physical plant and equipment value could easily support a $12 million mortgage bond, and Equitable insurance indicated interest. The difficult part was finding a large regional bank to split the remaining need for an unsecured term and revolving credit. Since this was a New England deal, my first move was to visit Bank of Boston. Dick Hill, Chairman, and Bill Brown, President, were bankers I knew well. We had been involved in past deals and were comfortable talking about mutually beneficial business. Bank of Boston was proud of its history as a secured lender to the leather and textile industries. Their loss record was reflective of their practice of factoring and commercial credit. Both Dick and Bill were interested in the Brockton deal, but they insisted on liens on inventory and receivables. I explained that such conditions would kill the Equitable bond.

A short walk across Federal Street brought me to Tom Trigg, President of Shawmut Bank, another Irving correspondent bank. Irving cleared letters of credit transactions originating at New York City piers, and occasionally participated in loans that exceeded Shawmut's legal limit.

Tom Trigg knew about Knapp-Kingsize and respected Win Short. He told me that Win was a director of Brockton Trust Company and that he was looking to expand Shawmut's business in that area. He listened to the proposal, introduced me to a senior credit officer, John Green, and took the financial information package we prepared and promised to get back. A week later, Mr. Trigg called to say Shawmut would participate for one half of the bank credit, $3 million. I discussed the financing with George Murphy and he agreed that he would be comfortable if Irving took the remaining $3 million loan.

Six months later, Louise and I attended a dinner party for important Northeast customers at the Irving Trust, suite 36H, at the Waldorf Towers. George Murphy and his wife were host and hostess for 20 guests, seated at a single dining room table with us included.

At the reception preceding dinner, Mr. Murphy observed that Louise was showing and on his fingers calculated that she most likely conceived in September on our Hawaii trip. Holding Louise's hands, he looked at me and said, "Don't you now wish that you ate all those peanut and jelly sandwiches?"

Louise commented it was nice that we brought a live souvenir home from Hawaii.

1970 was a great year. At the age of 39, I was appointed to a new position as Assistant Division Head, National Division, with six regional vice president district heads reporting to me. It was the year I was elected as Chairman of Group No. 8, the representative of New York City banks on the Board of Directors of the New York State Bankers Association. That year I was also invited to join the finance committee of the U.S. Chamber of Commerce in Washington, D.C.

Louise and Number Eight

That June I was scheduled to attend the annual meeting of the New York State Bankers Association at the Lake Placid Club. I remembered attending a black tie directors dinner meeting wearing a white dinner jacket and listening to speeches until 9 pm. Realizing that Louise was due to deliver back in New Jersey, I got into my car and after three hours arrived in Short Hills. As I drove up the hill to our house, I could see lights were on. When I walked into the house, Helen Coen, a neighbor and good friend, was there to look after the children. Her husband, Bob, planned to take Louise to the hospital in my assumed absence. Louise greeted me with the happiest expression of relief. She was packed and ready to go to Overlook Hospital in Summit. Wow! I made it. I always felt that there were two signs of a good husband. Number one was getting your wife to the maternity room on time and number two was getting your Christmas tree up straight.

Baby Nancy was delivered at 6 am on June 18th. While still wearing my black tie and formal white dinner jacket, I was instructed by Louise to go back to the house on Hemlock Road and find in the pantry a dozen helium-filled pink balloons to take to the Short Hills train station and greet Mrs. Stewart, our daytime maid, who would distribute the balloons to other familiar maids announcing the arrival of our eighth child, a daughter, Nancy.

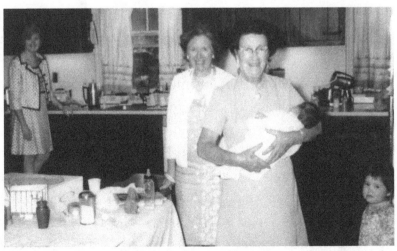

Christening day for Nancy with Louise, Bill's mother Beatrice holding the baby, and Louise's mother Imogene (Imo), with Margie in the shadows.

Out of balloons and still wearing my formal attire, I headed back to Lake Placid to have lunch with Arthur Levitt, State Controller, and play golf that afternoon with the State Treasurer. I couldn't wait to get some sleep.

Louise was an indispensable supporter of my entire career. She frequently drove from Short Hills into New York City to join me at dinner with couples from out of state. She had a marvelous memory for names, and could often remember and mention previous meetings. She was great at business related receptions, where we would greet hundreds of people in line as host and hostess.

She would post herself beside me with a, "Hello, Bill, you remember (so and so) from Kansas City (or wherever)." This teamwork was especially helpful when attending industry conventions.

Returning from such an event held in Miami, Florida, she mentioned having visited the Miami Diocese office while I was playing golf. She met with a Catholic Charities representative and explained that with eight children we were desperate to hire full-time, live-in help. Louise said, "Since Miami attracted refugees from Latin America, perhaps the Diocesan office might be of assistance."

Louise was told that the Miami office would help, but they needed confirmation of character from the Newark, New Jersey, Diocese.

When we returned to Short Hills a week later, Louise mentioned visiting the Catholic Charities Newark office. She told them that she would like arrangements with the Miami office and needed support from Newark. She was told that they had a better idea. It seemed that the Newark Diocese operated a home for unwed mothers. Young women in their eighth month of pregnancy were housed and cared for through delivery. Catholic Charities wanted to place them in the earlier months of pregnancy with respectable families. "What do you think?"

My response: "Listen, Louise. We just brought home our eighth child. Picture this: Every time friends come to our front door they're greeted by a different pregnant maid. I can hear them saying, 'It looks like Craig solved his problem.'"

We went to an employment agency. Because of our large family, we had a lot of live-in turnovers.

Price Wage Controls

At a meeting of the US Chamber of Commerce in Washington, D.C., the subject was growing concerns about inflation. The Chairman of the Council's Finance Committee was Beryl Sprinkel, the chief economist at Harris Trust Company in Chicago. He later became Chairman of the President's Council of Economic Advisors, appointed by President Richard Nixon. President Nixon was greatly concerned about the growing threat of inflation. The Federal Reserve estimated that the country had price inflation close to 5½ percent. Congress and the press were seriously suggesting price and wage controls. Our Chamber meeting heard all the pros and cons, but much to my surprise the committee seemed to favor controls. We were invited to testify before the Senate Finance Committee. When our committee chairman stated that the U.S. Chamber thought controls made sense, the Senate Committee Chairman remarked, "If the U.S. Chamber of Commerce agrees to the introduction of price/wage controls, why look for objections?"

My fear was: Once in place, how far might they be expanded? Limited price/wage controls were put in place in early 1971;

however, we shortly began hearing about Phase II price controls. I began wondering why I was bothering about issues unrelated to my job. The Bankers Association feared that if there were a Phase II, it might permit government to control interest rates. Soon I was requested to go to Washington and lobby congressmen to exclude loan interest from price controls.

I was assigned to visit Ed Koch, the future NYC mayor, who then represented the midtown Manhattan district known as the "Blue Stocking District." I had met Koch previously and always felt comfortable with him. An appointment was made, and I arrived on time.

He seemed in a hurry and said, "Bill, I'm awfully busy, and I'm behind schedule. What's up?"

"Ed, I'm here representing the New York State Bankers Association about the threatened ceilings on bank loan rates as part of Phase II price control legislation. "

"Bill, everyone is concerned about price controls. Yesterday a group of Texas cattlemen were here and I told them that if it was in the best interest of the American economy, Congress could direct when to raise the cow, when to kill the cow, and how much to sell the cow for."

"Ed," I said, "if I were here yesterday I would have told you about the young rancher, drafted to serve, climbing down the swinging ropes onto a landing craft at Iwo Jima, with enemy shells exploding all around him. Knowing his life was at stake, he didn't think he was doing it for some bureaucrat who was going to tell him when to raise the cow, when to kill the cow, and how much to charge for the cow." I felt puffed up by my clever statement until I noticed Ed's slight smirk.

He waited for me to finish before sending me on my way. "Hey, Bill, good story. You should have been here yesterday. Now, tell me about the banker at Iwo Jima." For many years after, whenever we met, he would ask about the banker at Iwo Jima.

FORMING A BANK HOLDING COMPANY

Throughout most of the country, bank regulation limited branching to within single counties. In 1969 the New York State legislature voted to allow statewide bank ownership via Bank Holding companies. Irving hired Oren Root, a former State Commissioner of banking, to head Irving Capital Corp. The Irving Trust New York State Banking Department reported to me. Root and I worked together to help expand bonds we had with upstate correspondent banks.

The first bank acquisition was Rochester Trust Company, whose largest industrial client company was an outfit that built modular houses. These factory built houses were produced as units assembled on site, and the units were moved around the country by train or truck. The operation was a godsend for public housing where foundations could be poured in the fall and finished houses could be assembled the following spring or summer. The indoor construction proceeded year-round. In the winter season, completed units were stored outside, covered with heavy plastic.

The president of the company was on the Board of Rochester Trust. Since the bank had seasonal loan requests from the company that exceeded their legal lending limit, a backup line of credit for $10 million was provided by Chemical Bank. Oren Root suggested that they shift the credit line from Chemical to Irving.

Because of the size of the loan, it required my sign-off. I was scheduled to accompany Jim Kuharski on a four-day trip upstate.

Jim, a VP, handled that area. I suggested we include a visit to Rochester Trust and the modular home builder.

Little did I know that Louise had asked Kuharski to get me out of town that week. She was planning a surprise 40th birthday dinner party for the following Friday evening. Louise and Jim agreed to have me home at exactly 6:30 pm. I certainly was surprised to find 40 friends in our second-floor playroom all seated for dinner.

Family picture taken on Bill's 40th birthday.

Cathy and Bonnie

Dede and Matt

Bill, Jr. and Ricy

When Jim and I visited the plant in Rochester, I noticed Armstrong Cork ceiling tiles and flooring in heavy use. I mentioned to my brother, Dennis, that I was impressed by my visit to our new account. He told me that his credit manager was planning an on-site visit to the plant. They were concerned about the size of outstanding and delayed payments. Den said that because of my interest he might tag along.

Subsequently I received a call from brother Den. "Hey, Bill, we have a problem. During our visit to the Rochester plant, my associate and I walked up a hill to a level area where finished product awaiting shipment was seasonally stored. There were at least two hundred units tightly wrapped with heavy plastic. They must have been sitting there for months. We checked inside a few and observed many warped connecting edges caused by condensation. These units wouldn't fit together when delivered to their destination. Frequently these modular homes are shipped to towns and cities for public housing. We returned to the company office and reviewed their accounting records to find that this finished inventory was carried on the books as sold."

George Murphy, Irving's Chairman, was very proud of his success; his holding company's first acquisition of an upstate bank. He was pleased to demonstrate how much local businesses gained when a financial center bank was brought closer. Mr. Murphy had already instructed the Public Relations Department to select pictures and write storylines for Irving's annual report.

After returning from my trip to Rochester and talking to my brother, I visited George Murphy's office. He was shocked by my report and stunned when I told him I would not initial the $10 million loan request. He inquired about my brother Dennis. I explained that growing up he was always the smartest one with better grades. He had better credit skills and experience than most bank-trained credit analysts. The loan was not approved, and within a year the company went bankrupt. The SEC sued management for fraudulent accounting.

"Thank you, Dennis."

Brother Den and Bill paired at a member guest golf outing at
Canoe Brook Country Club.

Dr. Joseph Haenn

In 1955, Dr. Haenn moved his family from Merion to Haverford, Pennsylvania, just down the road from Merion Golf Club. With the post-war economic expansion and the suburban housing boom, he had acquired Mehl & Latta in Rosemont, Pennsylvania, a town between Bryn Mawr and Villanova, a building supply company with large storage tanks for delivery of home heating oil in the area. He extended that business to a similar facility he bought in Malvern, about 15 miles west on Lancaster Pike. Both properties had several acres of land with railroad sidings. With the Haenn Lumber Company mills located in Center City, and the ship sealing business headquartered on 2nd Street near the Delaware River, he had a thriving business. Unfortunately, it was labor intensive and unions in these good times introduced contract terms that required expanded work rules; i.e., drivers only drive, a separate employee loaded delivery trucks, and another man rode along to unload. There were strict limitations about when workers could be put on temporary duty.

Dr. Haenn suffered from cancer for two years and died in 1966 at the age of 75. He spent his final months at Fitzgerald Mercy Hospital in Darby, Pennsylvania, run by the Mercy Order of Nuns. I visited him frequently while he was hospitalized. On one visit, he mentioned that his father had donated the land for the hospital, which is acknowledged by a plaque in the lobby. Looking out the window, he mentioned that his father had donated about one hundred acres that surrounded the hospital. He commented, "I doubt that my father would have been pleased to see that two fields across the road are now a cemetery. It seems that combining a hospital with a cemetery is a conflict of interest."

Joe and Bobby Haenn, Louise's brothers, were both in the family business. Bob was six years younger than Joe and decided he didn't want to spend the rest of his life working for Joe. He pulled up anchor and took a position with Smith Barney in their Philadelphia office. Haenn Lumber Co. and Haenn Ship Sealing were liquidated, leaving Mehl & Latta as a stand-alone business. The home oil part of the company was sold and the remainder was the suburban operations with the union contracts. The first downturn in the economic cycle brought serious losses. Joe had no control over labor costs, and his effort for belt tightening led to a strike and threats of property damage.

The company assets were held in Dr. Haenn's estate at Gerard Trust Co.

I joined Mrs. Haenn and Joe with family counsel in a meeting with the trust company executives. It was decided to leave the land holdings in the trust but finance the inventory and receivables, transferring the remaining company to Joe, a losing operation with heavy debt. The father's estate retained the proceeds of the inventory and receivable loans; the lending banks remained whole, and the trust retained valuable land.

The Rosemont property was subsequently leased to a shopping center developer, and the estate contracted for a percentage of revenue from stores that leased space in the center. The Malvern facility was sold.

All was not lost. After Mrs. Haenn died, the total estate when distributed to eight children after 55 percent inheritance taxes was not a bonanza, but it was a blessing for the members of this very special family. Joe Haenn, Jr. did not fail; he was dealt a bad hand.

Customer Entertaining

I served on the Board of the American Bankers Association, and while attending an Association annual meeting in Miami I was scheduled to host a dinner party for Irving correspondent bankers at the Sonabend Hotel at Key Biscayne. Paul Collins, the Southern District Vice President, thought that if Louise and I hosted the evening it might improve the draw.

The hotel was right on the beach with palm trees flapping in the wind. Louise was seated at the far end of a table set for 20, and I was opposite her. The seating arrangements were decided by Collins, placing me next to his best customers.

A bottle of wine in a slanted reed basket was placed on the table between the guests. The table had a lovely large flower centerpiece with rows of lit candles held on glistening silver stands next to the wine. As dinner was served, I reached for the wine basket near me and tilted it, asking my guest if he could make out the label in the candlelight.

He kindly replied without raising his voice. "Craig, I can't tell you the name on the label, but you're pouring wine on my lap."

After dinner I told Collins, "We owe him something."

With all my travel and entertainment, only twice was I questioned by the bank controller about charges to my expense account; $750 for fish and $900 for swimming lessons. I was happy to explain both.

The largest deposit account we had in the New England District was Travelers Insurance Company, headquartered in Hartford. The company maintained a deposit account of about $20 million. I couldn't identify any loans or services to justify such a large account balance. That amount was there at that level when I took over the district, and my job was to be sure it was there when I moved on. I visited the VP Finance and Treasurer twice and remembered them telling me about trout fishing in Maine. I remembered that Irving Michaels, the jeweler, had a large estate in Hamden, just above New Haven, with a large brook-fed pond stocked with trout. There was a log-built lodge with stuffed big game and trophy mounted fish. I had fished Sebago Lake with the Michael brothers, and the family agreed that I was welcome to have guests stay overnight and enjoy the place. They suggested that I bring down from Maine a fishing guide they used, who was great at telling stories around a fire pit. The only problem was that the pond fish population was down. I arranged for a ton of trout to be delivered but not fed for two weeks before my Travelers executives arrived. We all had a great time, and the account remained one of our best.

The swimming lessons had an easier explanation. At a West Virginia bankers convention at the Greenbrier resort hotel, the Irving Trust East Central District VP invited regional bankers to attend a reception at a large hotel suite where Louise and I would be at the door greeting guests. I was alarmed to learn that the bank staff members who made the arrangements were unaware that the Greenbrier was in a county with blue laws prohibiting the sale of liquor on Sundays, the day of the planned party. Not wanting to bring a group of bourbon drinkers to a tea party, I begged Greenbrier management to help find a solution to the problem. With a wink and a nod, I was told that if alcoholic beverage bottles were to be brought to the rooms we were using, the charge to my account would not be for booze but for something else; therefore, the $900 for swimming lessons.

NEW TOP MANAGEMENT

Both George Murphy, Chairman, and Bill Peterson, President, were scheduled to retire at about the same time, requiring the Board of Directors to focus on selecting successor management. Apparently the transition occurred without much forward planning. Arthur Boardman, who headed the International Division, succeeded Bill Peterson. Arthur had only a short time before retirement.

Joe Rice was brought in from IBM to move Irving into the computer age, and Gordon Wallace, who headed the Trust Division, was given a crash program in commercial banking. In a year's time, he shifted from loan administration through the collection department, to Vice Chairman; and when George Murphy retired, he became Chairman, but he too was only a few years from mandatory retirement. Joe Rice moved through all the administrative departments to become President. My observation was we lacked a commercial banker at the top. I became high on the headhunter lists, and these executive placement firms suggested several moves.

Energy and Minerals Division

As a reaction to the Yom Kippur War, the Arab countries aiming to penalize the West interrupted oil supplies from the Middle East and formed the cartel OPEC. Europe and the US were soon in short supply of all petroleum products. People lined up their cars for gasoline. It was the central topic across the country and around the world.

Wallace had retired, and Rice was in charge. I was asked to form a new division to be called Energy and Minerals. Obviously the country could no longer depend on foreign oil but should expand efforts to find, develop, and finance more minerals production.

I was off on a recruiting mission. While I was an experienced corporate lender, I lacked knowledge about oil and gas production, mining engineering, land leases, and royalty contracts. Fortunately I had a reputation for teamwork, and with the help of the bank's personnel department, I became immersed in job interviews. Within two months, I hired a petroleum engineer, a mining engineer, an attorney who specialized in royalty contracts, and two well-connected business lenders in the energy field.

It was now time to solicit business. I bitched until we got respectable office space on one of 1 Wall Street's upper floors. I had a private office on the ninth floor corner of the building at Wall Street and Broadway, overlooking Trinity Church, right under the Chairman's office. I was glad to give it up to join my new team. Had we not all moved together into upscale quarters, the group, new to Irving, might have questioned where they stood in the pecking order.

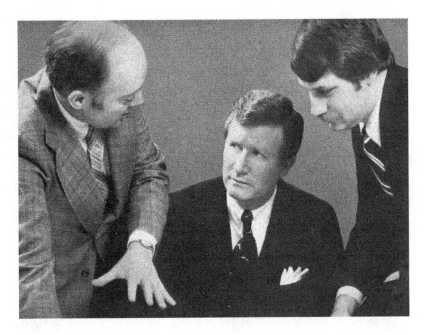

Bob Murdock, V.P., a petroleum engineer, and Bryan Taylor, V.P.,
a mining engineer, with Bill, analyzing a loan proposal.

Brian Taylor, a mining engineer from New Zealand, came over from Citibank; Bob Murdoch, a petroleum engineer, joined us from Shell Oil. The rest of the team had either practiced law in the oil and gas fields or came from investment banks or other commercial banks. I visited several investment bankers I knew to broadcast the fact that Irving was now in the energy and minerals business. John Childs, after retirement, joined Kidder Peabody with his friend, Al Gordon, who headed the firm. They invited me over for lunch. They wanted to hear about my plans for the Energy and Minerals Department. After I described my program to date, Al Gordon said, "Bill, I wish you well, but I'm already impressed that you attracted that guy from Citibank."

This became a real learning experience. I was accustomed to corporate credit evaluation and lending based upon balance sheet and income statements. Energy and minerals lending was primarily supported by project evaluation. Most project financing was structured upon estimated value of mineral reserves, the quality of the information, and completion guarantees from substantial sponsors. I learned it was folly to depend on a geologist report. A geologist might say that studies confirm the existence of geographic formations indicating a high probability for oil; however, he has no idea about how much and at what production cost. Petroleum engineers gather information from drilling reports that indicate size of reserves and likely production duration. Until 15 percent of estimated reserves are produced, the project is not bankable without the guarantee of a substantial producer. This rule of thumb has proved to be almost 100 percent reliable. But it takes a petroleum engineer to study the data.

Mining credit has a different pitch. Most mineral deposits located around the world are known. The success of a new mine, whether it be copper, nickel, bauxite, silver, coal, gold, or iron, depends on the ratio of overburden to ore, location, transportation costs, political safety, and price competition. Often these large projects require production rates in excess of a single company's needs.

The steel industry knew for years that the highest quality iron ore was in the Caracas region of Brazil. The ratio of extracted iron ore to removed overburden was better than any other world source; however, it wasn't touched because it was deep in the Amazon jungle, requiring a 200-mile railroad line with 70 trestles to bring the ore to port. This project was successfully completed, but long after I was in the business.

The same dynamics applied to a deal we did involving a well-known bauxite deposit at Rio de Norte, 1,500 miles up the

Amazon River. Brian Taylor had worked on other projects with CVRD, the largest mining company in the world. The company is headquartered in Rio de Janeiro. He learned that several aluminum companies were interested in forming a worldwide consortium to tap this rich source of bauxite. This was the perfect situation for project financing.

Brian told CVRD that if they could assemble major aluminum companies in the US, Canada, and Europe to participate with credit support, we would arrange to provide the development funds. CVRD came back with commitments from Alco and Reynolds in the US, Aluminum Co. of Canada, Norse Hidro in Norway, and Eni in Italy. After many engineering studies, estimated costs were agreed upon.

A 50,000-ton vessel tested the river's 1,500 miles during the dry season, and turned around. The feasibility of the project was confirmed. (The Amazon River delivers 20 percent of all fresh water entering the world's oceans.)

A town needed to be built near the mine site; docks, a rail system, and a plant to convert bauxite into alumina required construction money.

Construction members provided equity funds with guarantees. We structured a $200,000,000 loan. As lead bank, we took a $20,000,000 share plus origination fees, participating out the rest. Our agreement required sales proceeds (out of which we received debt payments) be paid in US dollars deposited at Irving Trust Company. In a side agreement, the borrower agreed to pay Irving a $2,000,000 fee if when things were up and running another group of banks or investors bid to take Irving out of the deal. I learned after leaving Irving, rates dropped, and, in order to take advantage of lower rates, the borrower paid off the loan and gave Irving the $2,000,000.

Project financing is a natural for money center banks. The only way two or more large companies can arrange to finance a major undertaking is by sharing the risk. Each company involved purchases shares in a jointly-owned company. The new company seeks to verify the feasibility of a project as beneficial to the partners. There must be agreement among the partners that they understand the risks and are willing to guarantee completion and to meet financial tests. The debt of the new company is off sponsoring company books, except the guarantees may show up in the footnotes. Until the project is completed and operations are profitable, the guarantees of bank debt stay in place. The credit judgment shifts from the borrower to the participating partners.

With project financing, we funded partnerships of major companies all over the globe: Indonesia, Africa, Alaska, the North Sea, Canada, and Southwest US.

While the team proved their worth, I personally enjoyed direct involvement with people I knew in the coal business.

Developing New Business

It's interesting how contacts made early in a career can reappear later. While in the Utility Department I formed a good relationship with Carl Horn, who was the financial vice president at Duke Power Co, headquartered in Charlotte, North Carolina. He proceeded to become Chairman of the Board. His passion was hunting for game birds. We met by chance in New York City and arranged to have lunch together at the Plaza oyster bar. He mentioned company plans to build a new coal-fired generating station near Winston-Salem. I asked if Duke had decided on a coal source.

He replied, "The coal supplier would be determined by furnace design requirements."

I mentioned that VICC had untapped mine reserves that might qualify. "The property is less than 100 miles north at Pulaski in Virginia."

A month later, Carl called to tell me that his purchasing people had visited VICC and, if they could open a new mine meeting quality and production requirements, they might be in contention for the business.

I told him that, if the new mine was dedicated to a firm contract, financing could be assured.

I mentioned to Carl that the Pulaski VICC property had a hunting lodge, trained bird dogs, and pin-fed birds of all kinds, ready to be liberated. I told him I'd mention our mutual interest in bird hunting to the VICC President and see if he could host us for a couple of days. "Call me if you can get away."

When Carl got back to me, we selected two days for hunting while staying at the lodge. George Holland, the VICC President, joined us.

The lodge sat on top of a hill surrounded by lawn edged with a country-style hickory fence. The rooms were comfortably furnished and a wood burning stone fireplace graced the living room. On our first day, we enjoyed walking the fields with the well-trained Brittany Spaniels who pointed and flushed up a variety of birds: chucker, quail, and pheasant. That evening the cook prepared and served a wonderful game dinner. Before retiring, we played gin rummy and George Holland asked if we would like to shoot ducks the next day.

Carl asked if we would need to get up at dawn.

"Where and when?" was my question.

Holland responded, "Anytime, right here."

The property had a large pond with caged ducks at one end

and feeding grounds at the other end near comfortable blinds. A red phone was used to notify an attendant to open one of ten cages and a dozen ducks would fly over our position. Before departing, a taxidermist took a few selected retrieved birds fit for mounting, and the rest were cleaned, dressed, frozen, and sent home for us. Carl was thrilled with our two days together and thanked George for the special treatment we received.

A year later, a Duke/VICC contract was signed and Irving Trust made the loan for building the mine and wash plant. The VICC story, which began with financing Bates Manufacturing Co., did not end with the Duke Power Co. deal.

One afternoon, Bill Koch, whom I knew from my Boston business days, came to my office. He informed me that he had formed a private investment firm called Oxbow and explained his interest in the coal business. Bill Koch was far less known than his brothers, Charles and David, who managed the family-owned Koch Industries headquartered in Wichita, Kansas. Bill cashed out of the family business, taking $600,000,000. He became better known when he skippered and underwrote an America's Cup racing yacht.

I told him about VICC and arranged for him to meet Ginsberg and Finkelstein, who now owned all the stock. After much back and forth, he acquired 51 percent of the company for $12 million. Within three years, he sold his interest to American Natural Gas Company from Detroit for $50 million. Bill decided to leave mining, preferring to broker coal for export.

Al Smith Dinner

I kept in touch with David Finkelstein and Arnold Ginsburg. Every year when we were living in the New York City area, we would go as their guests to the Al Smith dinner at the Waldorf. This annual dinner was a fundraiser for the New York Archdiocese. The Cardinal was always the Master of Ceremonies, and over the years the guest speakers were some of the most prominent people, including Presidents Kennedy, LBJ, Nixon, Reagan, and G.W. Bush. Entertainers such as Bob Hope, Groucho Marx, and Perry Como performed.

I noticed that most of the audience sat at tables hosted by Jewish couples. I thought it odd that Jewish support was so evident, and one evening I asked our hosts, "How did this come about?"

David Finkelstein, who was chairman of the board at the Brooklyn School of Law at the time and previously was a Judge, responded with a little-known story. "In 1947 the UN was considering establishing a homeland for Jews displaced throughout Europe during the war years. A motion was introduced in the General Assembly suggesting that a Jewish state be established in the Palestine Territory. The motion was voted down. Six Latin American countries voted no. Jewish community leaders, including Finkelstein, met with Cardinal Spellman, who favored the UN proposal. They asked him to share his feelings with his counterparts in those six countries in the hope that their governmental influence might draw support. The Cardinal followed up with a visit to South America and encouraged the UN to reconsider. The second vote had enough support to pass, and the road was cleared for the formation of Israel."

Those New York Jewish community leaders were unlike the gospel story about the thankless lepers that Jesus healed. Only one out of ten returned to say thanks. The Jewish leaders returned to Cardinal Spellman gushing with appreciation for his support. They wished to convey their thanks and offered to show perpetual gratitude by establishing an annual Jewish supported fundraiser for the NY Archdiocese, which became known as the Al Smith dinner. After more than 50 years, it's a tradition of repeating their thanks.

In 1978, Louise and I flew to Tel Aviv with Cardinal Medeiros, Archbishop of Boston. The group included four priests and six lay people. This was the first time in 30 years that a senior Catholic Church official visited Israel. The Vatican refused to recognize the government because the new country took ownership of church property. The Holy Land shrines were maintained by the Franciscan Order, but several office buildings and retreat structures in the cities were appropriated by the government. A settlement had been worked out, and a going forward relationship was in place. The Cardinal's visit was more symbolic than official protocol. We followed the path of Christ visiting shrines from Nazareth to Jerusalem. We met with government officials and spent time at Yad Vashem, the holocaust museum. We wondered at the economic progress of their new nation and the fulfillment of the world-wide dream of the Jewish people.

Carl Smith

I met Carl Smith at a coal industry convention. He had a small coal business headquartered in Charlottesville, Virginia. He had friends teaching at the University of Virginia mining school. He often commissioned them for consultation and advice. He learned about a family owned coal property with neighboring royalty mineral rights.

The land had been drilled and core samples analyzed, which indicated significant thick high-quality coal. Carl met the owner, who told him that he felt too old to open up new mines and at the right price would consider selling out. The property was called Black Mountain, near Beckley, West Virginia, with close-by railroad access.

He had learned about the VICC deal and wondered if I might introduce him to one of my power company friends. I told the story to the Chief Financial Officer at Southern Company in Atlanta. He told me that one of Southern Company's subsidiaries, Alabama Power Co., might be interested in looking at a cost plus arrangement. "Craig," he said, "you know the Alabama Power Co. management. Arrange for Smith to visit the purchasing agent, then have him call on Southern Company Services to see what they think about his sample cores and underground mapping."

Carl and his UVA mining school advisors presented his proposal to Alabama Power. After a month of study and negotiation, Carl Smith got an agreement to open a limited cost drift mine at Black Mountain with a minimum size wash plant. Southern Services gave a loan guarantee. If the pilot operation went well, they would consider agreeing to a project loan, thereby opening a full production facility.

Like the Duke deal, the project loan would have Alabama Power's guarantee for completion and the requirement to meet certain financial tests. When those events occurred, the bank loan would be paid out with proceeds from an insurance company using longer-term bonds. Banks avoided long term financing. It was 1973 when Carl Smith got this big break.

In 1974, my son Bill, Jr. was being considered for a basketball scholarship at the University of Virginia. Carl Smith, whose home was next to the campus, invited Billy to stay at his home when he visited UVA. Bill didn't get picked and settled as a walk-on at Villanova. Carl died in 2005. During his lifetime Carl Smith donated over $50 million to the University of Virginia.

Irving Trust wasn't big enough to lead mega projects, but when a big syndicated loan was structured by Citibank, Chase, or J.P. Morgan, we participated. We booked loans for the Alaska pipeline, a copper mine in Indonesia, and offshore drilling in both Norway and Scotland. While I was pleased that in fewer than three years our unit produced more than $200,000,000 in high quality loans, I still bristled about being shuffled off the senior executive track. I was distraught about the bank lacking a commercial banker at the top.

Louise bringing Carrie home from the hospital, our ninth child.

Shawmut Bank

Apparently, my feelings were noticed, and I received several job offerings. Placement firms suggested top positions at a few banks and arranged trips and visits followed by attractive offers. I had little interest in packing up my family and moving away from familiar turf.

An Irving SVP who headed the Public Relations Department commuted from Princeton, New Jersey, often sharing a train seat with a Paul Stafford Associates partner.

The headhunter learned that I might be approachable for the right opportunity. Paul Stafford Associates contacted me in

February 1976 with the suggestion that Shawmut Bank of Boston needed someone to dig them out of a portfolio of troubled loans. They were offering a title of Executive Vice President and a clear shot to the presidency.

Louise knew I had become frustrated with Irving and felt the Boston area would be welcome. I went to Boston and met with Tom Trigg, who since Larry Martin's recent retirement was now Chairman Tom Trigg. He was 62 and would be in that position for three more years. Logan Clarke had just been elected President. He was brought up through the ranks having been with Shawmut for 30 years. With the weak net income, the bank was showing he did not seem to have his position nailed down.

Shawmut Bank had a long-respected history of financing trade in the textile, wool, cotton, and leather industries. The Board of the bank included top management from those companies, plus the Chairmen of Raytheon, Gillette, John Hancock, and Boston Edison. The bank had been in business for over 130 years and in 1905 was the 10th largest bank in America. It was indeed a compliment to have a shot at the top of such a respected institution.

The decision to move from New Jersey to the Boston area was not what most of my family members wanted to hear. Only a year before we had added Carrie as our sixth daughter. For the rest of her life, she proclaimed her importance because, "We waited for her."

Pulling up 11 family roots wasn't easy. No matter how often I repeated that we were headed to New England to enjoy a better life, I got eyes looking skyward. Son Bill was a high school junior looking forward to being quarterback of Milburn High's football team and captain of the basketball team. On the day I planned to tell the family children my plans, I went to Bill's room before he got out of bed.

After I told him, I'll never forget what he did. He pulled his pillow over his head and yelled, "It's a bad dream. This can't be happening!"

Bill was given a choice of boarding in Short Hills for his senior year or moving with the family. I told him it was his decision, but I also pointed out that in following years whenever he returned from college for holidays and vacations he wouldn't have friends in the Boston area. My consolation speech didn't go over very well. That night was prom night. He was dating a senior. He took the car and his date with friends to Atlantic City overnight. He returned ready to stick with the family and move to Boston.

Prior to accepting the position at Shawmut, I gathered as much information as I could about the condition of the bank and its holding company. Top jobs do not go to outside search unless there is serious leadership and financial trouble. Considering the problems and actions taken to upright the business, I saw despair and opportunity. I wasn't blind to the risk of going with Shawmut Bank.

In 1973, three new executive vice presidents were brought up from the ranks along with a vice chairman. This group of executives headed retail and commercial banking: international, real estate, trust, financial control, market research, public affairs, and data processing. Every one of these senior officers was gone by 1975, along with three SVP support officers.

It was not until 1976 that the Federal Reserve could report some upturn in the economy. 1974 was a year of hardship and 1975 was no better.

Tom Trigg became Chairman in 1974, and while his backup executive team faded away, I was impressed with the actions he directed during these worst of times.

As 1974 opened, problems that began in 1973 gained momentum, with inflation and recession vying for center stage. Shawmut had an imbalance of long-term fixed rate loans. Most bank policies limit such bookings, preferring short-term working capital loans. Financing a portfolio of fixed rate loans with variable rate funding is costly when rates rise.

While the recession affected banks throughout the country, New England seemed to be hardest hit. In January 1974, Shawmut's ratio of classified loans (loans of questionable quality) to capital had climbed to 18 percent. Circumstances dictated closer loan review activity. Where collection possibilities were remote, such loans were charged off as soon as they were identified. The systematic write-off of loans required a correspondingly substantial increase in the reserves set aside for potential future loan losses. Banking rules required that such reserves could only be established through charges against current earnings. Shawmut had experienced slight loan losses prior to 1970. Based on that experience, reserve provisions were not enough to cover growing write-offs.

Shawmut realized this, and in 1974 and 1975 made substantial additions to the loan reserves. Coming all at once, these substantial charges had a drastic impact on earnings. Most of these provisions were made in the last quarter of 1975, creating a $5,764,000 operating loss for that period.

The loan-loss provision for the year was $22 million compared to $13 million in 1974. Corporate earnings were $1.5 million in 1975 compared to $15 million in 1970.

I took the job at age 45, after thoroughly analyzing the facts just mentioned.

I concluded that Shawmut took a lot of needed hard medicine, and having learned a great deal, would not just recover but prosper. I felt needed. What would keep the funds flowing to Shawmut was the bank's name and reputation.

There was one Shawmut action taken that I felt was a big mistake. Shawmut adopted the Overhead Value Analysis (OVA) program in 1975. An outside team of advisors was called in to work with senior bank officers in designing the overhead reduction program, and in early 1976 plans for such reductions were in place. The plan focused almost exclusively on staff reduction, although the second phase included reduction of non-salary expenses. Personnel cuts were to be based on a variety of factors, including level of performance and necessity of a particular job. The decision as to who would be released should be made by the division heads. Manager performance was measured by head count reduction, which led to panic. I was happy to have missed conducting these tribunals. As financial results deteriorated, pressure built to accelerate head count reduction and many people at all levels were let go, causing low morale throughout the organization. Three hundred and seventy people were released in one week, and March 1976 quarterly salaries decreased from 1975 by $2 million, hardly worth the effort. It most likely hastened the departure of the significant number of top management people.

Moving to Concord

Moving from Short Hills to Boston caused little upset. The Short Hills house on Hemlock Road was acquired in 1969 from a builder who acquired a large estate with subdivision in mind. The main house on the property was big and needed some updating, which he completed before putting it back on the market with two acres.

When we purchased this stone mansion, we had seven

children. In 1970, Nancy was born, and Louise delivered Carolyn in 1974. When I say big, each of the children had his or her own bedroom. The master bedroom suite had a fireplace, as did the living room, dining room, sitting room, library, and ballroom.

The Hemlock Road house still has the highest elevation in Short Hills. From second floor windows, looking east, you can see the Verrazano Narrows Bridge, which connects Staten Island to Brooklyn. Looking west about 20 miles, you can see Morristown Airport. On a few foggy days we called FAA to request that commuter planes and helicopters en route between Morristown and LaGuardia fly higher. My golfing children could walk down the street to Canoe Brook Country Club, and we had a tennis court in the back yard. There was a three-car garage and the driveway encircling the house was one-tenth of a mile. Anyone taking jogging exercise could circle the house 10 times for a mile run without leaving the property.

Selling the Short Hills house was no problem, but finding something similar in the Boston area was a concern.

We had three homes in Short Hills because our needs expanded, as did our family. We arrived there with two children and left with nine in 15 years.

A real estate consulting firm was engaged by Shawmut Bank to help Louise find our new home in the Boston area. It was hard to believe how many appealing locations were available: Center City, Cambridge, North Shore, South Shore, and western suburbs.

Louise stayed at the Ritz while being escorted about by a consultant who confused her showing so many attractive homes that were available. She had friends who lived in Lexington, Weston, and Concord, and when she was shown 153 Garfield Road in Concord, she was convinced it would be better for the family than the great place we had in Short Hills.

The owner descended from the family who founded Jordan Marsh. They had a race horse that won that afternoon at the Atlantic City track. After meeting Louise, they wanted to share their good fortune by reducing their price.

I love telling the story about this house. Jumping ahead in time, in 1988 our son Ricy arranged for a 30-foot flagpole to be set in the grass area in the center of the driveway circle across from the front door in celebration of the 300th anniversary when the first part of the house was built in 1688.

The Concord Public Library maintains a file about the house and its occupants, including drawings and photos after 1880. In 1720, Isaha Hosmer, a Puritan minister, attempted to walk across the frozen Concord River. He broke through the ice, never to be found. Mr. Conat, a Harvard College President, lived there, and in the mid-1800s, Henry David Thoreau referred to it as the Old House of Concord.

In 1895, the property was acquired by Theodore Dumaine, who removed most of what remained of the old house, which over the years came apart and was restored several times. Mr. Dumaine engaged a well-known Boston architect to design a large Georgian brick house, saving and restoring two rooms and preserving the stone walled cellar, the ground floor, walnut paneled colonial style sitting room, and a bedroom above. In 1905, the family moved into their 10-bedroom, 8-bath mansion with six chimneys, on 100 acres, with separate 3-car garage. Mr. Dumaine was wise to have included so many bedrooms, not that he had so many servants, but he and his wife produced 9 children. The oldest son, Theodore, Jr. (called Buck), inherited Amoskeg Mills, which was located on the Merrimack River. These were the largest cotton mills in America in Manchester, New Hampshire. He owned the Boston and Maine Railroad, Waltham Watch Co., and Fannie Farmer Candies. Buck acquired the Bangor and Aroostook Railroad and the Long Island Railroad.

Amoskeg endured severe labor troubles in the early 1950s, and Mr. Dumaine couldn't believe that with the concessions made regarding wages and working conditions that employees would vote to unionize and go out on strike. His management bargained for a year before he decided to close the New Hampshire mills and move south. Six thousand jobs were lost in New Hampshire. New mills in North Carolina and South Carolina were built under the name of Fieldcrest. Amoskeg later acquired Cannon Mills.

Mr. Dumaine, Sr. died in 1958, and by that time the stock held in each of the family-controlled businesses was transferred into a 100 percent owned Amoskeg company. His son Buck inherited Amoskeg, much to the dismay of his sisters and brothers.

It's intriguing that on stationery and on the front door knocker the house was named "Harmony House." While we lived there, Buck's siblings would come by to share childhood memories. By the time we bought the property, the grounds had been reduced to five acres, but a swimming pool and tennis court had been added. The building went through several renovations, and the furnishings from Short Hills proved more than adequate.

When we moved to Concord, son Bill was going into his senior year at Concord-Carlisle High School. Matt was a junior, Ricy a sophomore, Dede a freshman, Bonnie was in eighth grade, Cathy in seventh grade, Margie in fourth, Nancy was in first grade, and Carrie was at home, pre-kindergarten.

The Shawmut Bank Board of Directors Search Committee reviewed interviews conducted by outside consultants concerning my background. While I received high marks, there was much praise for Louise. Several Board Members told me later that readers of those remarks jokingly claimed, "Maybe we should be hiring Louise." They liked the idea that Louise would be a bonus.

It's almost impossible to imagine anyone filling Louise's job description. The move to 153 Garfield Road, Concord, MA required her reinvention, after having to give up her deep-rooted social involvement in Philadelphia and Short Hills and the comfort of being established, recognized, and respected there.

Starting all over, she had to resettle into her fifth new neighborhood, which required: house restoration, painting, decorating, landscaping, selecting service suppliers, and arranging for help. Caring for nine children was itself an overwhelming task: registering children for school, meeting neighbors, attending parent-teacher meetings, involvement with the children's school and sports activities, joining church and town functions, chauffeuring the kids all around, preparing school lunches, and putting dinner on the table every night for 11. Add to this routine, being on call to drive 24 miles from Concord to Boston to promote her husband's ambition: meeting with Bank Associates, entertaining customers, and attending civic functions. Louise took things as they came, as everyone she met marveled at how happy she was and how glad they were to be in her company.

Garfield Road, Concord

Each property on Garfield Road included several acres of land and woods. One estate belonged to Doris Kearns and Dick Goodwin. Louise and Doris were good friends, and occasionally we dined at home together. Doris is a famous Harvard historian, appearing frequently on TV regarding politics, having written several books about Lincoln, FDR and LBJ. When our daughter Diane (Dede) was preparing for her graduation from Concord - Carlisle High, she asked Doris to be the graduation speaker. Doris agreed. The ceremony was planned to be held outside on the football field. Wearing her academic robes, reflecting her liberal arts degree from Colby College and her MA degree from Harvard, she crossed the mud-soaked field in high heels only to lose her right shoe in the muck. Without breaking stride, she stayed in line, marching to "Pomp and Circumstance," and took her turn hopping to the podium. After the ceremony, under Louise's supervision, our kids found the shoe, cleaned it and returned it to her at home with cocktails.

Becoming President

Shawmut's recovery did not occur overnight, and much of 1976, 1977, and early 1978 were devoted to resolving problems that had surfaced during the recession and opening new areas that would be developed into the 1980s. In 1976, corporate earnings rose to $5.8 million. By 1977 the figure was $7.7 million, and in 1978 income had reached $10.1 million or $5.41 per share.

Toward the end of 1977, I reported to the Board of Directors on improvements made in the lending area of the business. They included moves to increase loan volume through expanding national credits, and by focusing on certain industries for business development. The loan review function was separated from credit analysis. The Equipment Financing and Leasing

Departments disbanded as part of recession cutbacks were revised. The Board was told about the expansion of our Collection Department and the successful recovery from written-off loans. In 1978, Logan Clarke had some job and personal conflicts and resigned as President. Tom Trigg then assumed both titles, Chairman and President.

Realizing that policy required his retirement in 1980, he recommended that a committee of directors be formed to determine his successor. In September, the search committee, chaired by Ed Matz, CEO of John Hancock Insurance Co., returned their findings that the committee unanimously recommended with full agreement of Trigg that John P. LaWare become the 16th president of the bank and corporation. Then in two years, upon Trigg's retirement, he would become chairman and I would become the 17th president of Shawmut Bank at the age of 49. In 1980, net income was above $24 million compared to $14 million in 1974. Instead of beating into the wind for six years, the wind was now at my back.

John LaWare became one of my best friends. A year after he arrived, he arranged for me to attend the Advanced Management Program for 13 weeks at the Harvard Business School. He and several Board members went to Harvard; he felt I should have the big H in my résumé.

During one of the final weeks at Harvard, while the class was seated in the declining rounded classroom where most case studies were discussed, the class was asked to consider and comment on a prepared new case study. It was a rare day when Dean Foracre sat through a session. The presenter who had written the case was not a Harvard Professor but an attorney from Chicago. It was a time when there was media focus on corporate managers' responsibility to the communities nearby.

The criticism at the time was that HBS was preparing future executives to make money without consideration of what they might do to support nearby community needs.

The general idea was that as a company policy some senior managements discourage company officers from spending some of their time supporting local charities and public institutions. The examples were Crown Cork & Seal and Connelly Container Co. John Connelly was the CEO and controlling stockholder in both related companies. The point was made that Connelly didn't want his corporate officers involved in such activities when they should be at the office. The presenter went on and on, casting aspersions on Mr. Connelly, making him out to resemble Ebenezer Scrooge in Dickens' story, *A Christmas Carol*.

When the presentation ended, Foracre took over and asked for remarks. Most of the responses were in one way or another, "I got the message."

I raised my hand and said, "Dean Foracre, I read in the *Boston Globe* a few days ago where Dr. Land, who founded Polaroid, gave Harvard $5 million. John Connelly gave my college, Villanova, $5 million last month. I don't know, Dr. Land, but if he discouraged his employees from charitable activities on company time, which he did, would you feel comfortable hanging him out to dry?"

Dean Foracre waited at the door and nudged me aside and said, "Craig, this case won't see the light of day, but we must get the point across that business success is not just about making money. HBS needs to shape a case that conveys the need for some level of community commitment."

The Dean asked me to join him for golf at Brookline the following Saturday.

My promotion to President of Shawmut was announced while I was living at the Business School in Cambridge. Warren Berg,

SVP Public Affairs, was instructed by LaWare to personally deliver a magnum of champagne to my room. I didn't take it home; we emptied it with the help of all the floor residents. It turned out that Warren took another magnum out to Concord for Louise.

As the new President, I was curious about the history of the bank and the story behind its unusual name. The bank was formed in 1837, and the name first appeared in 1630 in the *Charlestown Record* as the peninsula that Indians called Shawmut. In 1896, Charles Francis Adams published a Massachusetts history in which he discussed the meaning of the term "Shawmut," retelling William Bradford's early account, which described a 1621 meeting between Myles Standish and a local Shawmut Sachem called Obbatinewat, who had cooperatively signed an agreement with Standish opening the Boston area to English development. What could be more appropriate than to have an artist design a logo for the bank with a single head of an Indian? The image was created by Adelbent Ames, Jr. in 1910. In 1976, the year I arrived in Boston, the new bank headquarters was completed. It covered an entire city block: the Shawmut Bank Building at One Federal Street. The 38-story building housed the Downtown Harvard Club, serving noontime and evening meals to members and guests. The Club's presence in the building attracted a number of high quality tenants. The bank assumed 40 percent of the space available and the balance of the building filled out in two years. It was an address of distinction in the heart of Boston's financial district.

Community Activity

John Green, my Executive Vice President and senior loan officer at Shawmut, often said that lending money should be boring. There should be no excitement in lending other people's money. He was right, but I'd rather not finish this book telling boring stories. There are too many interesting stories associated with the opportunities one gets as a community leader.

Serving on boards of institutions with community ties was encouraged by Shawmut Directors. It may seem that writing about outside activities while limiting discussion about office work could appear unbalanced. There is plenty of excitement in office work and management. But assigning officers into and out of responsibilities, hiring and firing, making acquisitions, attending division and department meetings, visiting with key customers, loan approvals, and attendance at branch office promotions are necessary but dull to readers unless they are familiar with the people involved.

I helped to arrange for the acquisition of a large regional bank and a mortgage banking company. I became Chairman of the mortgage company and expanded operations into five additional states. I served on the Board of Atlantic International Bank, a merchant bank headquartered in London, which took me to Europe four times a year. I was a partner in American Ag Credit, which required me to be in Amarillo, Texas, three or four times a year. The Ag Credit Company financed cattle in feedlots throughout the southwest, with outstanding loan balances in excess of $500 million. We never lost a dime and I'm not going to let you in on our secret. In 1978 I was accepted as a member of the Association of Reserve City Bankers. Membership is limited to bankers headquartered in one of 12 cities in the US with a regional Federal Reserve Bank branch. Membership is also limited by the rule that only two executives representing banks with minimum assets of $10 billion may join. Membership included only 280 members, but it represented 95 percent of all bank assets in the country.

The group met twice a year; the winter meeting was always in New York City and the spring meeting was held around the country at upscale resort hotels. Over time I was a member of the International Committee, the Administration Committee, and I chaired the Golf Committee. As Chairman of the Golf Committee, I didn't realize it but I became kind of a power broker. In the mid-80s banks went headlong into merger marriages. At the spring meeting, I was responsible to arrange tee times. I felt I was collecting inside information when I was asked to arrange to have certain bank chairmen play together, aware that they wished to discuss prenuptial agreements.

In February 1978 there was an historic blizzard on the East Coast. When I arrived in New York City for a Monday and Tuesday meeting of the association, the snow was piling up. I stayed at the Plaza Hotel and by Wednesday nothing was moving. Rather than spend all day in the Oyster Bar, I arranged to do a walking tour of midtown Manhattan, meeting with membership committee members and friends in search of letters supporting my application for membership at the University Club. The snow kept building up, and, while you could hear snowplows clanging and scraping the streets, piles were so high one couldn't get off the sidewalk even if it was shoveled. I spoke on the phone with Louise, and she reported that the kids back in Concord, Massachusetts, were jumping out our second story windows into snowbanks. While we had electric lines along our tree-lined street and driveway, there was no power interruption. She reported that cars were snowed in and abandoned on Route 128, and Governor Dukakis put a curfew on all cars and trucks, banning them from the roads, with the exception of ambulances, fire equipment, and fuel vehicles.

"Honey, I'll be home for dinner tomorrow."

"How?"

"Trust me."

I called Penn Station and inquired about train service from New York to Boston. They answered that the rails were clear, and the trains were running, but what would I do when I got to Boston's South Station? I felt at worst I could walk to a hotel or sleep at my office. But I had a better plan. I called Billy Sullivan, who managed the Boston office of Metropolitan Petroleum, which was a Pittston subsidiary. Having checked the train schedule, I asked if he could have a home heating delivery truck at the station so I could avoid being stranded. I learned later that we needed an oil delivery, but I also managed to get home for dinner.

The Patriots

J. P. Routh retired as Pittston's Chairman in 1976, the year I moved to Boston. Nick Comecia became CEO. At the board meeting prior to J. P.'s retirement, he asked me to visit him in his office. He explained that the Metropolitan Petroleum Company Boston office was managed by Bill Sullivan, who was also owner of the New England Patriots football team. The team in the early years of the franchise played at Boston University Stadium and later at Harvard Stadium. Harvard chose not to renew their five-year contract but offered to extend the rental until the Patriots could find a new home field. Pittston directors offered to help Bill, and a REIT was formed to build a new stadium. The Pittston and Metropolitan directors agreed to provide one-third of the REIT financing, assuming a public offering would secure the balance.

J. P. said, "I would like to transfer the voting rights to you. Now that you are moving to Boston, provide Billy Sullivan your support and get us out of this."

Bill Sullivan was publicity director for Boston College, his alma mater, when Frank Leahy was the football coach. When Leahy left BC and became head coach at Notre Dame, he took Sullivan along with him to South Bend in 1942.

They left Notre Dame in 1947 and began a Hollywood movie production company called Sports Shorts. The product filled the gap at movie theaters along with: world news, travel, fashion and Bugs Bunny or Mickey Mouse. Bill wrote the script and Frank selected the topics. Film crews ate up most of the profits. In the late '50s they cut the Sports Shorts and left Hollywood. Bill returned to Boston and took a job with Metropolitan Petroleum.

In the late '60s, the NFL offered Frank Leahy the franchise ownership for New England. Frank wasn't interested, but he suggested that the offer should be made to his buddy Bill Sullivan. Sullivan purchased the franchise for $25,000, half of it borrowed. The REIT agreement would not allow the stadium to be used for any purpose other than Patriots football. The valuation of the stadium and therefore the REIT was simple, with receipts of 50 cents per seat in a 60,000-seat stadium, assuming sellout crowds for 10 home games comes to $300,000 per season.

The REIT stock was sold originally for $100 per share for 60,000 shares. With the REIT law requiring a pass-through of earnings to shareholders, the dividend in the best of times would be $5 a share. On a present value analysis, we're looking at a six million valuation. Sullivan contracted with Kidder Peabody's office to verify the valuation, and they hired Arthur D. Little to inspect the property. Our surprising finding was that all the toilets in the stadium drained into a leaching field on property belonging to a horse race course nearby and half the parking lot also belonged to the track.

I was pleased that a majority of the REIT shareholders voted to get out. There was an agreement to sell without the need to use my vote. With the ability to expand the use of the stadium and with the Patriots' right to increase ticket take by the stadium, the deal would be bankable. I told Billy that I felt too involved for Shawmut to make the loan, but I was pleased Terry Murray and Fleet Bank arranged financing.

I was named as one of four stadium directors, which offered little remuneration. We each had a one-quarter share of a director's skybox with seating for 16, plus kitchen. At the time, there were only two skyboxes: the owner's box and the director's box. The other three directors were long-term friends, and we had no trouble arranging for guests. As time went on and the team improved, ticket prices were increased and more skyboxes were added. The stadium name was changed from Schaffer to Sullivan.

Center: Bill Sullivan, introducing Bill Craig to an associate.

Pete Rozelle, Commissioner of the NFL, routinely increased the distribution of income from TV contracts, and the team went on to play in the Super Bowl in 1983. Chuck Sullivan, Bill's son, was an attorney and his practice included the NFL. He had the idea that stadium revenue could be greatly enhanced if they could contract for big-time concerts in the off-season. He sponsored the idea of having a Michael Jackson nationwide tour using NFL football stadiums in the league cities. Jackson's people thought it was a great idea. Don King was Michael Jackson's promoter (his great fame was promoting Muhammad Ali). Don King insisted that Jackson should receive a letter of credit guaranteeing they would receive $30 million. Thank God I wasn't asked to step up to that one. Chuck got the letter of credit pledging the team assets as collateral, including the stadium. What Chuck and Billy didn't realize was that Michael Jackson concocted a plan to have a 50-foot structure at the back of the stage for lighting, sound, and film images. This would restrict seating to about half of the stadium's capacity crowd.

Financially, the Jackson tour was a disaster. The letter of credit was called and the Sullivans were desperate. Billy didn't want to sell the team and proposed making a public stock offering. The NFL responded that the league partnership agreement prohibited a stock offering. When the Green Bay Packers issued stock, it was before the league agreement. A sale of the team required NFL league approval of any new owner. The Sullivans took the NFL to court, lost the case, sold the team and stadium, and paid off their bank loans. They made a bankruptcy settlement, enabling Bill to retain the respect and appreciation he earned for what he had accomplished.

Dorchester

I received a phone call from Kevin White when he was mayor of Boston. He explained that his office worked out an agreement with the Federal Housing Authority to provide term financing for a home for the elderly in a section of Boston called Dorchester on the Neponset River. The building had been a factory operated by one of New England's longest surviving companies, the Walter Baker Chocolate Co., founded in the mid-1700s. He explained that it was a solid brick building that if converted to living spaces would accommodate about 135 people. The conversion would require a fairly large construction loan.

I said, "It sounds good to me. I'll have our real estate SVP contact your assigned staff person and we'll take it from there."

About a year later, I got a call from Mayor White, who said, "The project has been completed and next Saturday at 11 am there will be an on-site opening ceremony."

At the appointed hour, I was sitting next to Mayor White on the stage of the building's auditorium.

He turned to me before the speeches and said, "Hey, Bill, many of the people sitting in the audience once worked in the Baker Chocolate factory. I can tell you who they are. They are the ones who lost their teeth."

Dorchester Heights is a hill above the town. History was made there in 1778. It was in the earliest year of the American Revolution. After the first battles at Lexington and Concord and the engagement at Bunker Hill, the City of Boston was under English military control. A group of patriots instructed by George Washington trekked through the woods for about 210 miles to Fort Ticonderoga on Lake Champlain. Control of the fort had switched sides from French to English during the French and Indian War, when Washington, as an English officer, served in the area. The fort was abandoned, but seven long-range cannons, which controlled ship passage on the lake, had been left in place. The patriots managed to remove the cannons and, with makeshift gear, took several weeks to drag the heavy equipment through the winter wilderness and ultimately placed the guns on Dorchester Heights overlooking Boston Harbor. The guns rested on the highest ridge closest to the harbor. From this vantage point more than 20 English warships were within range. A message was conveyed to the targeted fleet and demonstration shots were fired. The Americans gave the English a day to gather their soldiers, who assumed bedding rights in Boston, to load up and ship out.

The English fleet hauled anchor and left the harbor. A hundred years later, when Boston wanted to pick a day to celebrate this first victory of our Revolutionary War, there was consensus that the event occurred in March, but historians disagreed on which day in March. With the growing Irish population in the city, it was decided there would be a Massachusetts statewide annual celebration of Evacuation Day on March 17. Celebrants would drink green beer in honor of St. Patrick and the retreat of the British.

While thinking of Dorchester, I'm reminded of another happening. I was at my desk at Shawmut Bank when I received a call from David Nelson. He was Chief Justice of the State Superior Court and Chairman of Boston College. I got to know Dave well as directors of the Catholic Charities of the Archdiocese of Boston. He asked if I had time to hear a request.

"I'd be happy to," I said.

"Bill, I just got word that you were planning to close your Dorchester branch office. I'm sure you can justify the closing because it's a money loser. I didn't think it was any of my business until an incident that happened last night. I was honored at a dinner at the Parker House Hotel. There were hundreds of politicians and business people in attendance. I said a few words of appreciation and went out the front door with a large engraved silver tray under my arm. I was thrilled to be so recognized by such a highly regarded group of leading citizens. I decided that it would be nice to show my trophy to my mother, who still lived in Dorchester, where I grew up. There was a long line of cabs outside, and when I went to open the door of the front cab and mentioned that I wanted to go to an address in Dorchester, the driver got out of the taxi and said in a loud voice, 'I've been waiting in line here for half an hour, and I'm not about to take a black man to no black neighborhood. See if the cab at the back of the line will take you.'"

"Bill, I'm telling you this story because I've watched the town of Dorchester go down and down. I've suggested to my mother that she should consider a move. The only mixed racial business in town is your bank branch. Most stores are boarded up. There are a lot of fine black people living in Dorchester. But if they want to rent a car or apply for a job, they call your branch to get a confirmation that they are ok."

It didn't take me a second to respond. I remember I had wet eyes when I said, "Dave, I've never heard a better justification for keeping a branch open. It will stay open, and I will visit the Shawmut Dorchester branch office and let the staff there know how proud they make me feel about the important role they play in the community. As they say in your business, Dave, "Case dismissed."

Governor King and Tip O'Neill

In 1982 I was invited to join the Board of Directors of the New England Council for Economic Development. The board included the governors of Massachusetts, Rhode Island, New Hampshire, Vermont, and Maine. The Executive Director was Edward King, who had been in charge of the Massachusetts Bay Transportation Authority, which included Logan Airport. He had played for the Buffalo Bills football team, recruited after starring as a lineman for Boston College. He was well connected politically and right for the job. We became good friends. In 1983 I was elected Vice Chairman of the association. Traditionally the chairmanship rotated among the governors. That year there were several issues involving New England with federal agencies. The states were jointly anxious to continue dredging Boston Harbor to expand dock access and use the fill to extend Logan Airport runways.

Bob Page, CEO of Leesona Corp.; Maurice Segall, CEO of TJ Maxx;
John LaWare, Chairman of Shawmut; and speaking, Bill Craig.

King suggested that I accompany him on a trip to Washington to speak with New England congressional representatives. I remember taking Ed Markey to dinner. It was his first week as a Massachusetts Representative, and he seemed overwhelmed. Today he is a senator.

Flying back to Boston, King said he was thinking about running in the upcoming Democratic primary against the sitting Governor Michael Dukakis and asked me to chair his finance committee. I told him that as a new resident of the State I couldn't risk all the political slander that might rub off on the bank. He agreed but asked me to register as a Democrat. Ed went on to win the primary and the election.

At the same time, I had been appointed Chairman of Catholic Charities of the Archdiocese of Boston and became a close friend of Cardinal Medeiros. I really think I got that position because he was fond of Louise. Ed King won the election in November but would not take office until early January.

Similar to the lighting of the giant Christmas tree at Rockefeller Center in New York, in early December Boston had its tree lighting and caroling event at the Prudential Center. Having been held up at the office, I arrived late. Rather than taking a place behind the crowd, I went into the Prudential building because I was aware there was vacant space on the second floor. The only light came from the window facing the lighting celebration. Vision around the room was interrupted by structural blocks separating areas planned for future private offices, causing deep shadows across this large room.

Looking out, I could see assembled nearest to the tree the Cardinal, the mayor, many corporate big shots, and Ed King. While King won the gubernatorial election in November, he would not take office until the following January 8th. After a

136

while my sight adjusted to the darkened spaces around me. I could make out a figure behind one of the structural blocks. It was a fairly short well-dressed gentleman.

When he turned and saw me, he said, "Hi, Bill. How come you're hiding up here?"

It was Governor Dukakis.

"I might ask the same question, Mike. I was late and didn't want to be seen pushing my way to the front of the crowd. Louise is here and I was dropped off expecting to ride home with her when this event breaks up."

Mike responded, "I got here in time, but I noticed Ed King lining up with the honored guests and didn't want to pretend to be friendly or look like an also-ran. My driver dropped me off with the understanding he would return in 45 minutes. This is the most gruesome three-quarters of an hour in my life."

I've never seen anyone so depressed. I couldn't just walk away, so we stood there making a little conversation to break the silence.

Ed King

Little did we know that in three years Dukakis would win the nomination of the Democratic Party to run for President of the US.

Governor King was a good friend of US Speaker of the House, Tip O'Neill, who in my Irving Trust days borrowed a rather small amount to qualify as a founding director of the new Everett Bank Co. He had paid off the loan and resigned his position just prior to the bank's failure. He questioned that some of the big loans were made to fellow directors.

In the early '80s, energy costs were rising, and coal producing properties were selling at a premium. Tip O'Neill had a fellow congressman who represented a Florida district, suggest that he knew someone who owned a mine in Kentucky. The mine could not expand without a power company contract to pledge as collateral for a substantial loan. If Tip could introduce the idea to the New England Electric Co. and get his friend Ed King to go along, the three of them would be rewarded with stock options in the expanded mining company.

When Governor King got the message, he felt that it was not a career risk that Tip should be taking, no matter how great the reward. Ed asked me to talk to Tip as a coal guy and a banker. We arranged to play golf at Oyster Harbor Club on Cape Cod the following week. Tip had a house on the Cape in Chatham. I basically told him that every power plant had individual coal quality specifications. Rarely are the furnaces designed for coal sourced from a single coal seam. Often a blend is required. Even the senior management is unlikely to provide that information. It would most likely require having samples analyzed by the purchasing department, and you wouldn't know how many people would become suspicious.

"Don't pursue it. I admire how you avoided embarrassment regarding the Everett Bank. Don't gamble with your reputation."

Neither Ed King nor Tip O'Neill brought up the subject again.

Little Sisters of the Poor

Governor Ed King phoned me and suggested we get together for breakfast. He wanted to explain a situation brought to his attention by Tip O'Neill. "It might take all morning to solve the problem, so pick a day next week when you might be able to spare the time."

I said, "If it's a fundraiser, I'm not interested."

"Bill, I'm looking for your ideas."

"Ed, it looks like next Wednesday morning is clear. I'll be at your office at 8 am."

We met in his office Wednesday and he outlined the problem. Charlestown, Massachusetts was part of O'Neill's district. OSHA (Occupational Safety and Health Administration) was about to give notice condemning the residences for sick and elderly run by the Little Sisters of the Poor. Apparently OSHA inspected the hospital's main building and noted that the facility built in 1895 had wooden support beams and flooring, poor wiring, unsafe emergency exits, and therefore was a high fire risk. O'Neill said he was not in a position to override OSHA, and he wondered if we might have an idea to help.

Ed had arranged for us to visit Mother Superior, who had 12 nuns at that location, who greeted us warmly. After we toured the building and were impressed by the private rooms and cheerful dining facilities, we explained our agreement with OSHA that something needed to be done to correct the fire risks.

The sister in charge was hoping that some political pull would leave things alone. Ed suggested that they engage a contractor and architect to determine if the building could be restored and at what cost, offering an alternative to demolition and rebuilding on their very large well-located lot.

When I got home that evening, I explained the situation to Louise, telling her how difficult it would be to finance such a project and mentioning the questionable source of repayment. I told her I was shocked to learn that if the sisters needed to continue, they would raise the money by begging. I recall seeing them sitting on the top step of the stairs to the subway, hat in hand, wearing their traditional habits. I asked Louise how she would feel if one of our girls chose such a career.

She said, "Bill, I doubt if any of our daughters would shoot so high."

Paris Trip

Governor King was approached by an executive from Pan Am Airlines seeking support to lease an on-off gate at Logan Airport for flights to Paris, France. Ed had been responsible for Logan before he became Governor. He asked me about similar requests from American and United. I suggested he speak with Sam Pryor, retired Pan Am president, whom I knew from the Pittston Board.

About six months later Pan Am got the slot. There was a big fuss about celebrating the first Pan Am flight between Boston and Paris. Ed King was invited, and the food was to be cooked on board by the chefs written up in the movie, *Who's Killing the Great Chefs of Europe?* Ed suggested that Louise and I take his place on the flight. We had a great time for three days in Paris with Harry Taylor and his wife. Harry was a syndicated columnist and US ambassador to Switzerland.

Pro Bono – Director Services

Serving on boards of institutions with community ties was encouraged by Shawmut directors. I was Chairman of the Board of Massachusetts Higher Education Assistance Corp. (MHEAC) that oversaw the administration of bank and government guaranteed student loans, including packaging such loans sold to the Student Loan Marketing Association, (Sallie Mae).

I had a close relationship with Charles Adams when he was chairman and I was President of both the World Affairs Council and the United Way of Eastern New England. Mr. Adams, a great, great grandson of John Quincy Adams, was a retired chairman of Raytheon. Charlie was a most respected Boston gentleman. No one would refuse or fail to return his phone call.

The World Affairs Council met mostly to hear reports from

ambassadors and government leaders. Many speakers were Prime Ministers who were in Boston at the invitation of Harvard, Tufts, or Boston College.

Bill Craig greeting Brian Mulroney, Canadian Prime Minister at World Affairs Council luncheon.

These dinner meetings were held for as many as 150 members at hotel conference rooms. Written questions were selected and submitted to our guest speakers by one of us, who also made introductions and enjoyed conversation with the guests at the head table. It was a great opportunity for business people to share an interesting evening with their husbands and wives.

The United Way of Eastern New England coordinated fundraising from the largest employers with several offices in the area between Rhode Island and Maine. It avoided having United Way people from several towns and cities calling for annual donations when the effort could be centralized by a single contact with the main office. Our organization succeeded by getting high-ranking executives to volunteer to make those calls.

One such volunteer was Ron Burton, who would be scheduled to speak to assembled employees, encouraging direct salary deductions as a way to contribute. Ron was a Senior Vice President at John Hancock Insurance Co.; he had been an All American running back at Northwestern University and a first draft pick for the Patriots. He was a well-tailored, well-groomed, black, talented speaker. When Ron Burton spoke, people listened.

While I was Chairman of the Board of the Catholic Charities of the Archdiocese of Boston, I recruited Ron to become a Director, after introducing him to Cardinal Law. Over time I learned that he had his own special charity, which was a summer camp for inner city boys ages 12 to 16. The camp operated for five weeks a year on a 50-acre property west of the city. The program was divided between sports and studies. The sports programs included football, basketball, swimming, baseball, and track events.

Ron, the football hero, was there every day the camp was open. His motto was, "Learn to be sweet; you knock someone down, give him a hand and help him get back on his feet." In the studies part of the program for math and science, teachers stressed computer training. These kids often got into trouble after school when no one was there to keep an eye on them. Ron felt, come summer with nothing to do, the boys would find trouble. When Cardinal Law heard the story, he asked to visit the camp. Upon seeing so many young well-behaved boys wearing their white tee shirts and tan shorts, he promised to arrange and pay for 30 boys selected by pastors of inner city parish schools to attend the camp. It was a win-win.

Cardinal Law invited me to become a Director of the Saint John Seminary of the Boston Diocese, which was located on 60 acres next to Boston College on Commonwealth Avenue. The Board included six bishops, two theology professors, a nun, and me. You guessed it; I was to be Chairman of the Finance

Committee. At one of the Board meetings, I was scheduled to submit the budget for the following year. When the agenda called for my presentation, Cardinal Law looked down the table and asked if I would hold off discussing the budget; he wished to use my allotted time with what he felt was important — "Evil." If not evil, I thought having a shortfall of a million dollars in the budget was important.

At another time, a group assembled at the seminary to hear from a visiting Cardinal from El Salvador. The meeting was focused on the need for US reaction to the killing of eight Jesuit priests and the murder of Bishop Romaro while on the altar saying Mass.

When the meeting ended, Cardinal Law took my elbow, nudged me aside, and asked if I planned to attend the Red Sox game that evening at Fenway Park. It was 5 pm and the Red Sox were playing a World Series game starting at 7 pm. The Shawmut skybox had been assigned to Ted Hansberry, EVP head of retail and branch divisions. Law apologized but went on to impress upon me how baseball was so important in Central America and the visiting Cardinal would be eternally grateful if he could get to see a World Series game. I told him I didn't know if there was room in the box, and without tickets, how did he expect to get past security?

Cardinal Law said, "There are Sandinista sympathizers outside our front gate protesting the visiting Cardinal. There are two police cars keeping an eye on them. I could arrange for the police to enter through the back gate and take us to Fenway Park."

"And then what? I've got my car and driver waiting for me downstairs," I said. "There's a phone in the car. Let me see what I can do." I called Hansberry to see if he could make room. He agreed to squeeze them in. I then called John Harrington, trustee of the Yawkey estate and owner of the Red Sox. He suggested that if they would arrive at Gate C he would have someone there to let them in.

Law was back at his residence when I pulled up at the front door. He was wearing a Red Sox jacket. I said, "I've arranged for you and your guest to be escorted to the Shawmut skybox."

"Bill, I knew you would help us out. Can you join us?"

"No, Louise is holding dinner."

The first thing I did when I got to the office the next day was call Ted Hansberry. "I'm sorry, Ted, to have filled your box last night with a couple of clergymen."

"Bill, the customers loved it. You know our box is next to the owner's box. Mrs. Yawkey came over with a couple of her Hollywood guests, and the mayor and governor came over as well. It was great, except for one thing."

"What was that?"

"The Cardinals arrived with two policemen, and the cops ate all the shrimp."

An important customer and Shawmut Director invited me to become a Bentley College Director. It became apparent that anyone associated with the school — alumni, professor, student, director— had reason to be proud. Bentley became a university on my watch, and it has become known as one of the best American business schools. Our daughter Cathleen earned her MBA at Bentley, and I was thrilled to stand beside the President, wearing my academic robe, and handing Cathy her well-earned degree.

Living in Concord, Massachusetts, and having nine children to care for, I was pleased when our neighbor, a physician and Harvard Medical School Dean, nominated me to serve on the Emerson Hospital Board located in Concord. I learned something about the hospital business. As a not-for-profit hospital, Emerson is dependent on foundation contributors for updating and expanding. While I was a trustee and chairman of the Finance Committee, we added two stories to the main building and built a three-story garage, expanding parking by

150 places. I learned about getting permits for certain diagnostic equipment and how some doctors look for ways to form groups to own the machines, seeking extra income outside the hospital. As Chairman of the Finance Committee, I became involved in a union negotiation with the nurses. I hated seeing normally nice, pleasant nurses frowning at me when we passed in the halls.

"Hey, I'm here pro bono, and this isn't fun."

Both sides were pleased with the settlement, but I didn't stand for reelection. The job took too much time.

The memory clock brings me to the time to tell my favorite story. It wasn't a compliment from a high-ranking clergyman, a government official, or a big successful executive, but instead special recognition from the most respected, smartest person I knew: my mother-in-law, Imogene Felin Haenn (Imo).

I got a telephone call from my mother-in-law, whom I always respectfully called Mrs. Haenn, who said, "Bill, I have a decision to make and I would like your input. Members of the Board of Trustees at my college, Trinity, have contacted me suggesting they would like to put your name in as a candidate for nomination to the Board."

My sheepish response was, "Wow, what a compliment; however, it could only occur for one of three reasons."

"What could that be?"

"First, I would look good pictured in your annual report, with my youthful appearance."

"And?" she asked.

"Secondly, my acclaimed position in business might be impressive."

"And?" she repeated.

"Third, the school might think that my acceptance would be followed by more generous contributions from my mother-in-law."

She responded, "Forget the first two."

It was indeed an honor to serve on the Trinity College Board.

The college had been founded a hundred years earlier and provided Catholic women with equivalent education and sophisticated social bearing as any of the New England sister schools, such as Wellesley, Smith, or Mount Holyoke.

Recent graduates included Nancy Pelosi, Democrat House Speaker, and Obama Administration Health and Human Services Director, Kathleen Sebelius. Two of my daughters, Diane and Bonnie, went there, and I was happy to present them with their degrees. It was a pleasure to fly to Washington monthly to attend board meetings. My arrival was the social event of the week, as our daughters arranged for grill-room dinners for a dozen classmates to join me for a night out. I remember nights having beers at Bryn Mawr bars when I was at Villanova, but these girls enjoyed the same spirit with a bit more upscale level of discussion.

Mrs. Haenn, while not serving on the Board but having been president of her class, was included in Board of Directors dinners. We often dined at either the Congressional Country Club or the Chevy Chase Club.

At one of these occasions, she nudged me aside and said, "Bill, I'm uncomfortable having you respectfully call me Mrs. Haenn. Here among my friends I'm known as Imo. Please use that name in the future."

Hallelujah! How many sons-in-law know what to call their wife's mother? Well, I never liked the formal title "Mrs. Haenn." I became bold enough to say, "Imo, if I refer to you by that name here in Washington, I expect to do the same when back in Pennsylvania."

"I wish you would, Bill."

I couldn't wait to get back to the Haverford House in Pennsylvania to use my new prerogative in the presence of the other brothers-in-law. "Imo, would you please pass the salt?" I would be surrounded at the dinner table with lifted eyebrows.

INTERNATIONAL DIVISION

Part of the plan for Shawmut Bank stabilization was contraction of the International Division loan portfolio in Latin America. Many South American countries had severe balance of trade problems. Dollar loans were not being serviced, causing severe work-out and write-off problems for U.S. Banks. In the hope of negotiating improved terms of several loans, I agreed to accompany the head of our international division on a trip to Central and South America: Mexico, Venezuela, Brazil, and Argentina. We planned to fly from New York. The night before departure, Louise and her mother joined me for dinner at the University Club, following a meeting of the Knights of Malta.

Imo gave me an envelope containing $500.00 in $10.00 bills with instructions to distribute it to the poor while on my trip. In Mexico City we met with government financial people, correspondent banks and domestic customers. We primarily were in business districts and upscale neighborhoods. My 10-dollar gifts were few and far between, but poverty was not out of sight. In Brazil we stayed at a Sheraton Hotel on Ipanema Beach next to the Copacabana in Rio de Janeiro.

I had some spare time and took the tram above the city to visit the outstanding statue of "Christ of the Andes" overlooking the bay and Sugar Loaf Mountain. Our Rio business meetings with bankers and corporate executives were inconsequential. We were advised that questions could only be answered by the director of finance in the capital city of Brasilia.

We flew there and met with the Finance Minister, who

basically said, "Get in line."

We moved on to São Paulo, a city with the largest population in the hemisphere. Our accommodation was world class, but while the poverty was widespread, there was little opportunity to distribute the largesse from Imo. Guilt was setting in and I realized I wasn't fulfilling my mother-in-law's request. An afternoon was free and after spending time handing money to street peddlers, I decided to relieve my burden by visiting a center city Cathedral to see if I could get a little help. Walking up the main aisle, I was overtaken by an usher unrolling a red carpet. I was caught in the beginning of a wedding service. I couldn't get near the Priest, who was busy with the exuberant wedding party.

I noticed a man standing at the edge of the confusion who was wearing a multi-buttoned cassock with roman collar. I approached him. Not understanding Portuguese, the native language, I pulled out the cash envelope, handed it to him, and said in English, "For the poor."

He opened it, looked at the contents, knelt down, and with head bowed, said, "Thank you."

To this day I have no idea who received the money, but I hope it went from God's hands to the poor. Fearing failure and disappointment, I never told Imo that story. We spent the next three days in Buenos Aires in Argentina. The city is most like the best architecture you might find in large European cities. Most of the people are descendants from immigrants from Italy and Germany. The climate, the natural resources, and farming productivity are reflective of rich soil and abundant moisture. Raising livestock on the pampas produces some of the best cattle, sheep, and hogs in the world. God blessed Argentina with great potential, but the country has a devil of a time with politics and government.

It was not a good time to be in Argentina. Political opposition leaders were disappearing, business leaders were held for ransom, and security services were unreliable. On our way from Buenos Aires to the airport, we were stopped in our chartered car, held at gunpoint, and searched. I didn't know who they were, what they wanted, or what they would do with us. Without any explanation, we were allowed to proceed to the airport. I'm glad I was no longer carrying Imo's cash.

Every two or three months I travelled to Europe with a senior International Division executive. I needed to be in London for Atlantic International Bank Board meetings. I was also Chairman of a computer graphics company, Tech Export, which sold equipment through offices in every major country around the world. France, Germany, and England were central to our marketing. Although we had offices in Hong Kong, Tokyo, and South Africa, my travel to these offices was limited due to low revenue volume.

I was asked to chair a fundraiser for the Boston Symphony Orchestra (BSO). The BSO is composed of four parts: Symphony, Pops, Esplanade, and Tanglewood. By definition the parts of the BSO perform seasonally. The same musicians play throughout the year. The Symphony performs at the Symphony Hall in the city in December, January, February, and March. The Boston Pops also performs there in April, May, October, and November. The BSO is on the Esplanade in June and at Tanglewood in The Berkshires for July and August. This is the best seasonally managed orchestra in America. Because of the year-round employment of the musicians, their income is the highest, and their talent is tops.

The biggest annual fundraiser for the Boston Pops is the annual "Presidents at the Pops," held one night during an orchestra appearance. It is a prestigious event, with invitations to major company CEO's, and attendance is limited. The Symphony Hall is cleared of chairs, and dining tables and chairs are arranged surrounding the center of the floor.

The attire called for was black tie for men and appropriate gowns for the ladies. Typically, seating was arranged according to the size of the donation. Had I not been in charge I'd be placed in the back of the room. Louise and I were seated at the head table, set for six, including John Williams, the conductor, with his wife Samantha, and the BSO Chairman and his spouse. Boston was fortunate to have such a musical genius as conductor of the Pops. He was respected worldwide for the music he provided, including for the film, *Star Wars*; and everyone marvels at the music he composed for *Fiddler on the Roof*. He has been nominated for 50 Oscar awards. Only one other person has had more nominations; Walt Disney had 52. I remember we talked about thinking while avoiding distraction. Samantha said, "John could spend hours in isolation, getting his thoughts together."

After the dinner service was cleared, I stepped to the microphone to say a few words of welcome and appreciation and to introduce John Williams. The BSO came on stage and John suggested everyone stay seated while a five-foot layered cake carried aboard a round table covered with a white linen cloth flowing to the floor was wheeled to the center of the ballroom. John Williams announced, "Before we have any dancing, may we see Bill and Louise dance to the Anniversary Waltz?" What a great way to celebrate our 25th wedding anniversary.

As we circled the floor, I whispered in her ear, "There is an Old Milwaukee Beer add that says, 'It doesn't get any better than this.'"

Left: John Williams and Samantha Williams
Far right: Louise and Bill Craig

Time Out

Salmon fishing on the Bonaventure River in New Brunswick, Canada

Sailing from Northeast Harbor, ME to Marblehead, MA
on a Hinkley 49-foot yawl.

Pittston Company

In 1974, the year before departing Irving Trust, I joined the Board of Directors of the Pittston Company. I was introduced to the nominating committee by Fred Kirby, a director. I first met the company chairman and president when I was inquiring about Virginia Iron Coal and Coke (VICC).

Pittston started in the coal business around 1900 in the area between Scranton and Wilkes-Barre, Pennsylvania. The product was primarily anthracite (hard coal). Anthracite was most popular for home heating, due to its high BTU (British thermal units) content, producing very little smoke.

While there was plenty of coal in the region, most coal seams were uneven, requiring extraction by pick and shovel. Donkey carts were used to deliver coal from the underground tunnels. Ventilation was poor, ceiling supports were not uniform, and accidents were many. In 1920 the Pittston Coal Company acquired mines in the Southeastern United States to produce bituminous coal, which had a wider market for making steel and feeding utility boilers.

The Kirby family had a controlling interest in Pittston. The family were long term Wilkes-Barre people. Fred Kirby's grandfather started a five and dime business in Wilkes-Barre and ultimately partnered with F.W. Woolworth from Lancaster, Pennsylvania. He subsequently took control of the combined business. The Kirby's became financial giants through the family controlled investment firm, Allegheny Corporation.

In 1950, control of the Chesapeake and Ohio (C&O) Railway was purchased by Allegheny Corp. The firm specialized in railroads, including control of the New York Central. Alan Kirby, Fred's father, arranged to spin off C&O's coal property, merging it into the Pittston Coal Company, providing substantial reserves while expanding the operation to 40 mines in Virginia, Kentucky, West Virginia, and Tennessee. The railroad retained much of the business of moving coal from the mines to steel mills, navigable rivers, and ocean ports. Alan Kirby recruited a long-time friend, J.P. Routh, to run the company. Pittston's President, Nick Comecia, was a mining engineer from West Virginia, who had years of experience in mining.

The coal business profits permitted Pittston to invest in unrelated businesses: Brinks, Metropolitan Petroleum, New York Warehouse Co., and Burlington Air (BAX), a next day heavy freight airline. The combination was traded on the New York Stock Exchange as the Pittston Company, with corporate headquarters on Park Avenue in New York. Fred Kirby succeeded his father as chairman of Allegheny Corp. and chairman of F.W. Woolworth Co.

The United Mine Workers of America (UMWA) History

In the 1940s, the UMWA, led by fiery John L. Lewis, could boast of some 600,000 dues paying members. Its coalfield strikes paralyzed the nation. He defied a wartime ban on striking, and it took a threat by FDR to send in the Army to get the mines reopened. At the time, the UMWA was affiliated with the Congress of Industrial Organizations (CIO). Lewis, disappointed by the lack of support from the National Labor Organization, withdrew his union from membership in the CIO. The UMWA remained independent of the AFL-CIO for over 40 years; meanwhile, the Coal Miners Union shrank to fewer than 65,000 members.

Mining coal was commonly perceived as a dreadful way to earn a living. People cringed at scenes from the movie, *How Green Is My Valley*. There was fear of working deep in the earth, relying on helmet light, concerns about overhead supports, pumped air supply, constant water leakage, methane gas, and loud machine noise.

I felt my first concern as a director was safety for the miners. I was comforted to find out that every director felt the same way. It was common practice for each director to go underground annually with a mine crew to listen and observe employee concerns. A director felt it was more an obligation than an adventure.

In 1980, 52% of all electric energy produced in the US came from coal. The steel industry relied on coking coal to produce structures that form city buildings, railroads, bridges, cars, and appliances. Blast furnaces require a ton of coke to make a ton of steel. The labor component in coal production is essential to the economic success of the US; however, management responsibility, development of resources, equipment maintenance, and capital investment are equally important.

Bill entering a mine shaft.

Underground in a mine.

Only 20% of Pittston's coal production went to power plants; the balance was used for making steel. The company coal reserves contained the country's largest supply of high fluidity metallurgical (MET) coal, and Pittston was the biggest exporter of blended coking coal. A blend would combine the high fluidity product with production from three or four other company mines, blended at computer-controlled railroad car hump yards. High fluidity coal was a requirement in the blend prescribed for Japanese steel plants, rebuilt after WWII. It was known as the Pittston Blend. Pittston Coal Co., although relatively small, was the largest supplier of MET coal in the overseas spot market, competing against worldwide producers. MET coal contracts averaged less than one-year in duration. By comparison, power company coal providers delivered under long-term contracts, which had provisions enabling them to pass through cost increases.

Coal Industry – Economics

Prior to 1970, coal mining costs were 60% labor and 40% capital. In times past, having production equipment idle two days a week was a concern, but under later conditions, it was a big drag. Today the opposite is true, when coal mining costs are 40% labor and 60% capital cost. An example of this industry cost shift occurred in 1982 when, after geological and engineering studies, Pittston decided to go after a deep seam of quality coal.

The company named the mine Grand Badger. Since the seam held a modest amount of pyretic waste, it was necessary to add an on-site wash plant to the project. The total capital cost, including mining equipment, came to $46,360,000. The workforce required 61 miners. Capital costs came to $760,000 per mine employee. I attended a directors' picnic lunch at the official mine opening. I still keep a commemorative small pocketknife in my sock drawer as a reminder of the business risk in mining. The knife is engraved with the name Grand Badger.

The mine ran into serious floor and ceiling conditions above and below the seam, and the project was abandoned. The scheduled workers were absorbed into parallel jobs in the company. The company shareholders assumed the loss. When productive seams dwindle and expire, it's necessary to develop new mines and add expensive new mining equipment to retain production levels and hold market share. There is a constant need for more capital investment. The skills required to operate advanced equipment justify higher salaries.

The burden of increased capital investment rests with management, not employees. You would think a miner would rather operate a computer-driven machine than rely on his own strength. In order to justify the high equipment cost per miner, it is necessary to be in production more than five days a week. Saturday production is suspended for repositioning and repairs and Sunday is a day off.

Pittston wanted to provide for volunteer overtime and arrange for a Sunday shift. Such a move would increase the number of employed union miners, stabilize operations, and overcome losses. It wasn't just employee head count that was affected by mechanical progress; the company had to adjust to higher capital costs.

The UMWA said no to both suggestions.

Pittston bought another coal company, Paramount, which the UMWA failed to organize. Paramount, with its less restrictive work rules, included a Sunday shift. Pittston chairman, Paul

Douglas, was convinced that his company didn't need the BCOA (Bituminous Coal Operators Association), which was the industry group that bargains with the UMWA.

Paul Douglas succeeded Nick Comecia, former CEO, who had been chairman of the BCOA two years before his retirement. Douglas was recruited from the large international mining company, Freeport-McMoRan, where he was President. Paul's father was an Illinois senator, as was his grandfather, who was famous for having debated Abraham Lincoln.

Bituminous Coal Operators Association

In 1974, Pittston joined the 15-member Bituminous Coal Operators Association (BCOA), which negotiated one uniform UMWA contract for all its member companies. It was expected that non-BCOA members in the coal business would "me too" such agreements. In February 1988, the Pittston/UMWA contract expired, and the company withdrew from the BCOA, saying it was a different kind of company and needed a different sort of contract. Pittston wanted to negotiate separately. Most of the BCOA member companies were in a different business than Pittston. Eighty percent of BCOA companies contracted to produce coal delivered to power plants. Only 20% of Pittston's coal went to utilities. More than 50% of BCOA coal was produced from Midwest surface mines sold under contract to power companies. Regulated utilities have fuel adjustment clauses in their customer rate base. Fuel cost increases can be passed along to the power company's customers.

Richard Trumka, the UMWA President, became unhinged when the Pittston Coal Company exited the BCOA. The United

Mine Workers union membership had dropped drastically in recent years, as did the union share of US coal production. The US Department of Labor Statistics records showed that UMWA-produced coal in 1975 accounted for 70 percent of the US total; by 1988, it was 35 percent. The union claimed that Pittston was the only large coal company refusing to sign a BCOA/UMWA contract. In fact, in 1988, UMWA miners produced less than 40 percent of the coal mined in this country. During that period, total US production increased from 650 million tons to 952 million tons. The growth in tonnage reflects the growth of non-union production.

The industry found that union rules were too rigid. But if Pittston negotiated an agreement different from the BCOA contract and less favorable to the UMWA, it would be a disaster for the union.

Between 1974 and 1988 there was considerable advancement in coal production equipment. Investment in such equipment caused many small mining companies to exit the business. Modernization improved output and reduced manpower need. Over time the withdrawal of companies and employee early retirement caused a rapidly growing group of unemployed UMWA members drawing benefits from BCOA funds. Former employees no longer contributed to the fund. Sixty-five thousand active dues-paying employed UMWA miners were less than half the union membership. Another 76,000 members were either unemployed or retired. More than half the benefits paid to union members went to non-dues payers. The UMWA Benefit Fund was underfunded and showed poor investment results. Pittston wanted to assume managing its own fund for employee obligations, but the union insisted that the beneficiary pool include union members who never worked for the company – another issue never mentioned in media reports.

The union suggested that the company, by leaving the BCOA contract, would cause a loss of pension protection. Pittston's offer was more generous than any UMWA plan, offering portability, and was fully protected by law. The union also claimed that retirees would be left without medical benefits. The UMWA did not disclose the fact that in their proposal for a new collective bargaining agreement, the company offered a medical plan that would cover retirees as well as active employees.

Healthcare costs were an issue, since the BCOA industry-wide agreement provided 100% coverage. Pittston proposed to give every miner on their payroll $1,000 on January 1 every year, with the understanding that the first medical bills per family would be paid from that amount. If any of that $1000 was not used, the unused amount could be pocketed; any medical expenses over $1,000 would be paid by Pittston. The union refused because the BCOA agreement didn't include such terms. The company found that one of the reasons insurance costs were so high was that family members were allowing non-relatives to use the insurance cards for medicine. Students were lending their family insurance cards to college dorm friends.

Pittston Coal Company wanted to operate their mines six days a week and for more than 7½ hours and five days under current contract limits. The company wanted to add additional union employees and/or pay overtime to employees who so chose. An extra day of equipment use would significantly improve productivity and support survival.

The UMWA resented that the company allowed non-union contract miners to produce coal on some Pittston reserves through royalty payments. The union wanted to include a condition in the Pittston contract that would require such contractors to hire only union miners. The company would have trouble leasing out otherwise unused property if such a restriction were included in these leases. The UMWA wanted the company to discontinue this practice and include Paramount miners under this contract.

UMWA Strike

The UMWA members walked off the job at 40 Pittston mines in Virginia, West Virginia, Kentucky, and Tennessee on April 5, 1989. In June the union dropped out of negotiations. In July the union said it would negotiate with the help of a federal mediator, an effort that previously had failed to end the strike. The UMWA believed its strike against Pittston was an unfair labor practices dispute, while Pittston said it was merely an economic strike prompted by the company's refusal to sign the BCOA national labor agreement. Trumka was hoping he could get union supported politicians to join his side. Democrats from congressional committees visited the coalfields but only offered verbal support. Republicans in the then Bush Administration stayed clear. Jay Rockefeller, a Democratic senator from West Virginia, was quoted often in support of the union but short of proposing legislation. He was only a union sympathizer encouraging his base.

In July 1989, UMWA miners went on sympathy strikes in the eastern United States. Of the 65,000 active union members, 40,000 abandoned their work to show support for the Pittston strikers. Violent demonstrations spread throughout the coalfields. Trumka did not discourage this work stoppage, and court injunctions were handed down, leading to several hundred thousand dollars in penalties imposed on the union. After two weeks of these wildcat strikes, Trumka was confronted by many unauthorized strikers who received no financial support from the union, while official strikers employed by Pittston received living allowances from the UMWA strike fund.

Most local and national press and media reporting focused on the financial burden suffered by the miner families and their communities. Articles stressed the lack of social justice and greedy out-of-state companies. There were very few reports on the issues that separated the two sides.

Federal District Courts were busy issuing fines for damages and injuries caused by strikers. Many striking miners were jailed. Governors in those four states volunteered to serve as arbitrators, but they were ever present in the media, defending actions by state police who were brutalized by strikers while attempting to protect private property.

Director Intimidation

Trumka decided to shift focus away from the issues and go with a slick propaganda campaign replete with innuendo, distortions, and falsehoods aimed at Pittston directors, by recruiting clergy, the media, and any donation-seeking politician in a director's area, to make social justice the real issue.

I couldn't understand the logic of director intimidation; threatening a director's reputation in his community. It was made to appear there was a lack of sympathy for the oppressed, the poor, the vulnerable, unemployed, or as Hillary Clinton called them, "the deplorables." Obama referred to them as "People who kept hold of their guns and religion." The theory, I think, was that the director might want to correct that fabricated perception by making a statement or taking an action to advantage the union. When I was a Counter Intelligence Agent, this action was called recruiting a double agent. Having been Chairman of Catholic Charities of the Boston Archdiocese and President of the United Ways of Eastern New England, and having received a leadership award from the National Association of Christians and Jews, it wouldn't make sense to say I was insensitive to community and people needs.

Trumka felt he could compromise at least one of the nine Pittston directors.

Receiving award from National Association of Christians and Jews.

Directors:

Boston, MA	Bill Craig	Vice Chairman, Shawmut Bank
New York City	Bob Stone	Chairman, Kirby Oil
Corning, NY	Roger Ackerman	Chairman, Corning Co.
Seattle, WA	Gerry Greenstein	Chairman, Delta Airlines
Short Hills, NJ	Mark Anton	Chairman, Suburban Propane
Juno, FL	Jim Broadhead	Chairman, Florida Power & Light
Morristown, NJ	Fred Kirby	Chairman, Allegheny Corp.
Darien, CT	Jim Barker	Private Investor, Director, Verizon
Cambridge, MA	Carl Sloane	Harvard Professor

Alan Greenspan was on the Pittston board for eight years, prior to becoming Chairman of the Federal Reserve Board.

I refused to meet with Richard Trumka or his staff members. It would be out of line for me to be used, or to appear to assume authority that was legally in the hands of management. I avoided meeting with the press, fearing that I might be quoted or misquoted implying that a board member was not in concert with management. It was more amazing that the coal mine workers believed that by heavily donating to Democratic fundraisers they could expect regulatory support for coal company employees and coal country towns. It was apparent that political donations to party candidates from Green Conservation groups were louder, and coal was sacrificed on the altar of Global Warming.

Coal is the only mineral produced in America independent of foreign imports. The country depends on its use for 45% of our electricity. Most coal reserves suitable for mining are known; however, extraction requires many different production methods. State and federal regulation approval is required for every mine site. Surface and underground extraction approvals are time consuming and often subject to change. Regulatory delays and uncertainty make financing with long-term capital more and more limited. One thing is certain: existing mines will peter out and power plants will be converted to natural gas, no matter how much the UMWA union dues are spent for political action.

Trumka realized that the future was bleak. He saw that if he failed to bully Pittston to a favorable outcome, his career ambitions would be ended. He longed for a senior position with the AFL-CIO.

Trumka Pledges to Return the UMWA to the AFL-CIO

John L. Lewis, the UMWA boss in the 1940s, withdrew the UMWA from the CIO and was independent prior to the Pittston strike. Trumka approached the AFL-CIO leadership with the proposal that if the AFL-CIO would support him in the Pittston strike, he would arrange to have the independent UMWA return to the AFL-CIO. This accounts for the sudden growth in union picketers active in Boston striker demonstrations. There were thousands of AFL-CIO members in the streets: electrical workers, the pilots union, the hotel workers, the teachers union, the metal workers union, etc. All were making their presence known, wearing military camouflage outfits with UMWA patches. As many as three hundred cars traveling at 15 mph would hold up traffic for hours, with banners and signs reading, "Craig – Shawmut – Pittston neglect people and community needs."

My home in Concord, Massachusetts, had such parades, frequently blocking our road, and a platoon of army fatigue clad strikers made camp at the gate end of our driveway. One morning our daughter, Margie, was stopped on her way to school. She drove back to the house, called the police, and waited to be escorted around the picketers.

Following that incident, the police required the strikers to limit their presence at our home from 9 am to 5 pm. They could carry hand-held signs and could stand but not sit on the grass or the road.

Meanwhile Trumka was busy in search of political support. He met with Mayor Flynn and Governor Dukakis; he was interviewed on TV and submitted op-ed columns for the *Boston Globe* and the *Boston Herald*. Both papers avoided noting an understanding of the issues involved, but in editorials they disagreed with Trumka's effort to slander me. Knowing the publishers and editors of both papers helped.

Trumka and allied local union leaders attempted to arrange a meeting with Cardinal Law. He had little trouble finding high profile peace and justice clergymen to arrange a meeting. Law turned him over to a trusted assistant, but he kept me advised.

The union pursued Bob Stone, a Pittston director and Commodore of the New York Yacht Club, while leading a club summer cruise to Maine. He was met by strikers as he stepped ashore on the Northeast Harbor Dock. They were wearing army camouflage outfits and carrying UMWA signs. Fellow club members and crew laughed them off the pier.

The only fruitful director pursuit turned out to be with the ambitious Boston pols. Boston is a sports town, and the media dwells on most encounters as having winners and losers. The amazing thing was that there was little or no coverage on TV or in the press about issues differences. It was all about Craig/Shawmut and the unions. There were dozens of inputs from the AFL-CIO union leaders and a series of quotes from clergymen anxious to explain which side God was on. There was a deluge of opinions about the fairness and morality of attacking Bill Craig and the Shawmut Bank.

It wouldn't take an outside consultant to pick where the union could do the most damage. Boston, Massachusetts, the intellectual "Hub of the Universe," was the AFL-CIO center for New England. Every Democratic politician counted on union campaign money. The governor was a Democrat, both senators were Democrats, the mayor was a Democrat, and all city council members were Democrats. With all of them on your side, "What's there to lose?"

Self-interest of Boston Politicians

Mayor Flynn described Craig as a fair-minded man with a social conscience. Flynn also said, "I have a tremendous amount of respect for Mr. Trumka." This fellow can't lose. "I like them both, but there's more personal advantage to punish one."

The city council formally supported striking Pittston miners in a vote in July, approving a hearing encouraged by the UMW as part of the union's plan to pressure companies with interlocking directorships. The hearing was held on a day of planned protests at Shawmut's One Federal Street headquarters. The so-called impartial council members were all present, with Trumka waving agreement with the assembled AFL-CIO union members.

Richard Trumka appeared along with the Massachusetts AFL-CIO president, Arthur Osborn, at the Boston City Council hearing, considering a bill filed by City Councilor David Scondras to withdraw city funds from Shawmut Bank. Trumka conferred with Mayor Ray Flynn and the following day met with former Governor Michael Dukakis and State Treasurer Robert Crane to urge the state to pull its funds from Shawmut. While visiting with the former governor and state treasurer must have made Trumka feel he was on a roll, it led nowhere. I had served on finance and energy committees for the governor, and Bob Crane's wife, Mary, was my vice chairman when I chaired the board of the Catholic Charities of the Archdiocese of Boston. We were good friends.

Shawmut spokeswoman, Lisa Antell, said neither the bank nor Mr. Craig had any comment on the Pittston strike. "We are not a party to the dispute. Mr. Craig was associated with Pittston long before he was associated with Shawmut."

Apparently Trumka was also busy with federal politicians when the general counsel of the National Labor Relations Board ruled that the strike was caused by "Pittston's unfair labor practices, refusing to bargain in good faith, and that it had unlawfully discouraged its employees from engaging in union activities."

The ruling, if upheld, would prohibit Pittston from hiring permanent replacement workers. However, the ruling would not affect contempt court orders and fines that had been levied against the union for failing to order its striking members back to work. Pittston could not understand why the UMWA leadership was conducting an expensive media campaign against the company when Pittston's offer was better than the most recent contract signed by the union. Looking at the issues discussed, there didn't appear to be justification for a 12-month strike.

The missing roadblock to agreement was the union's insistence that Pittston rejoin the BCOA or "me too" with the most recent BCOA contract terms. Sixty percent of the country's coal mining contracts with the UMWA were based upon industry-wide terms; however, if Pittston negotiated a better package, then other mining companies would seek the same. It would split the BCOA, and the union would face multiple separate contract negotiations. If such were to occur, some industry analysts saw it breaking up the union and marking the end of Trumka's ambition.

Boycott of Shawmut Bank

Trumka returned to where he was most welcome, the Boston mayor's office. He met with Mayor Flynn, Council President Christopher A. Iannella, and Councilor David Scondras.

The UMWA had targeted Shawmut and eight other institutions nationwide, whose officials also sat on the Pittston company board. There was no other community or political reaction to the union's attempt to associate other directors or their companies with the Pittston strike. Only in Boston did union-supported Democratic officials jump at the chance to demonstrate to their union base for personal political gain. In mid July, Boston Mayor Raymond L. Flynn traveled to Virginia for two days to let UMWA members know they had his support in the Pittston dispute. "I want to let people know the treatment of the workers here was not appreciated by people of the City of Boston," Flynn said. He characterized himself as a long-term friend of the labor movement.

On July 19, 1989, I met with Boston's Mayor Raymond Flynn in his office. David Scondras attended the meeting. Flynn began the conversation by saying, "Bill, I've known and respected you for a long time. There's nothing personal in this proposed action regarding the withdrawal of City funds from your bank."

I interrupted. "Ray, what do you mean 'nothing personal'? You're willing to pressure me for your political benefit. It couldn't be a more personal attack if you clubbed me."

Flynn replied, "I haven't signed off on the City Council proposal to withdraw Boston City deposits from your bank, but I have to show the unions that I was able to get a statement from you that you have some sympathy with the striking Pittston employees."

"Ray, if you want a statement, I'll write it down." He handed me a piece of his stationery and I wrote: "As a director of the Pittston Company, I am concerned that a settlement take place which is fair and equitable."

Louise and I attended a Washington, D.C. prayer breakfast while we were there for an American Bankers Association board meeting. The principle speaker was Elizabeth Dole, then Secretary of Labor. After the breakfast, we met with Mrs. Dole, and Louise mentioned that I was a Pittston director. She and Louise discovered common interests, and Mrs. Dole confessed that the Pittston strike was a major concern of hers. She also stated she would soon announce the designation of an arbitrator in the hope of finding a settlement. A week later, William Usery, a former Secretary of Labor in the President Ford administration, took the assignment. I doubt if our meeting had any bearing on Mrs. Dole's action.

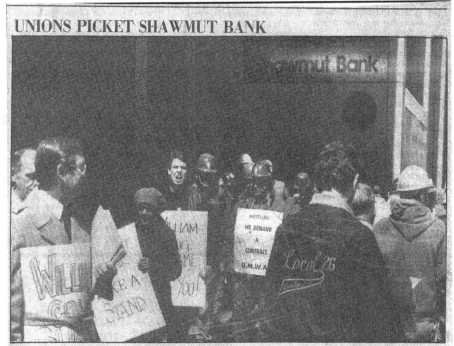

UNIONS PICKET SHAWMUT BANK

Globe staff photo/George Rizer

Boston labor union members protest outside of Shawmut Bank in downtown Boston yesterday, opposing Shawmut's ties to the Pittston Co. The unions charge the Connecticut conglomerate has forced a strike and disrupted the lives of thousands of coal-mining families in Appalachia. Shawmut vice president William Craig is on the board of Pittston.

The *Boston Globe* Article - 7/14/89

Boston Globe – July 14, 1989 headline – "UMW seeks help from Mayor Flynn and former Governor Dukakis":

UMW President Richard Trumka yesterday met with Mayor Flynn seeking support in the union's four-month-old strike against Greenwich, Conn-based Pittston Co. Trumka also spoke at a Boston City Council meeting about the link between Pittston and Shawmut Bank – one of Shawmut's directors, William Craig, is a Pittston director. As Shawmut's downtown headquarters were picketed yesterday, six of 13 City Councilors agreed to consider withdrawing City funds from Shawmut if a meeting between the UMW and Shawmut is not arranged by next Tuesday.

Boston Herald – July 14, 1989 headline – "UMW targets Hub Bank official": Trumka met yesterday with former State Treasurer Robert Crane and former Governor Michael Dukakis to urge them to withdraw state funds from Shawmut unless Shawmut Vice Chairman resigns as a Pittston director.

UMW President Trumka discussed the union's targeting Shawmut Bank with reporters yesterday. When asked, "Is the policy of attacking companies with interlocking directorates a new one for the UMW?" he responded, "We've done it before, but I don't think we've done it with the earnestness we're doing it now." The next reporter's question was, "What is the ultimate goal of coming here? Is it to get the City of Boston to remove its funds from Shawmut Bank, assuming there is no response or cooperation from Shawmut?" "Yes," Trumka replied. "Our goal obviously is to get support for the union." (Note: Craig couldn't be reached for comment yesterday.) Lisa Antell, a Shawmut spokeswoman, said, "Shawmut has no dealings with Pittston. Having checked our records, we find no current accounts or banking relationship with them. We have no involvement regarding the current labor dispute between Pittston and the UMW. We don't believe it's appropriate to comment on labor relations to which we have no relationship."

On July 19, 1989, I met with Boston's Mayor Raymond Flynn in his office. I was accompanied by John Hamill, a Shawmut senior officer. I needed a friendly witness present to avoid being misquoted. David Scondras, a City Council member, sat in at the meeting.

The next day, the Boston Herald newspaper quoted Scondras as saying that I caved at the Flynn meeting and promised to do things contrary to anything discussed. I'm glad I had John Hamill with me. Scondras claimed that I agreed to issue a statement within a week calling for face-to-face bargaining between the head of Pittston and the Union. He also bragged in the article that he got me to commit to call for a Pittston board meeting to discuss the labor dispute; and that I pledged to resign from the Pittston board if these suggestions were not acted upon.

Scondras said further in the article that the City Council would proceed to order a withdrawal of City funds from the Shawmut Bank "if not satisfied with the progress (Craig) reported to us on Monday."

The article and my response, written that day, are to follow. It mentions that Boston Mayor Flynn, with some national political ambition was traveling to Virginia, West Virginia, and Kentucky to demonstrate his union support without any concern about the issues.

So what was his reward for such dedicated union political support? Ray Flynn was appointed Ambassador to the Vatican, often referred to as an opportunity to buy lunches and dinners for monsignors and bishops. The highlight of the assignment was pictured years later in the *Boston Globe* showing Flynn in a drizzle, holding an umbrella over Bill Clinton; as the President arrived in Rome to meet the Pope. "What a reward."

---

42 The Boston Herald, Thursday, July 20, 1989

BUSINESS

WILLIAM F. CRAIG
Calls for bargaining

Council pressures Craig into action

By PHIL PRIMACK

A BOSTON City Council order to pull city funds from Shawmut Bank was delayed a week yesterday after bank vice chairman William F. Craig agreed to take public action regarding the Pittston Company's bitter coalfield labor dispute.

Craig, a Pittston board member, agreed to issue a statement within a week calling for face-to-face bargaining between the head of Pittston and the United Mine Workers union, according to city councilor David Scondras.

Scondras, who proposed the order to sever the city's ties with Shawmut as a protest against Pittston, said Craig will meet with the city council on Monday to describe actions he has taken.

According to Scondras, Craig will call for a Pittston board meeting to discuss the labor dispute. Craig pledged to resign his Pittston post if his suggestions are not acted upon, Scondras said.

Craig, who met with Scondras, city council president Christopher Iannella and Mayor Ray Flynn just before yesterday's scheduled vote, could not be reached for comment.

Scondras said the council will proceed to order the withdrawal of city funds from Shawmut "if we are not satisfied with the progress (Craig) reports to us on Monday."

Meanwhile, Flynn was to fly to the Appalachian coalfields today to meet with striking miners and supporters.

Unaccustomed to being slandered

Shawmut
William F. Craig
Vice Chairman

July 20,1989

Mr. David Scondras
Boston City Council
City Hall
Boston, Massachusetts

Dear Mr. Scondras:

I was dismayed to read in this morning's "Boston Herald" an account of our meeting yesterday in Mayor Flynn's office. The statements which you attribute to me are not only inaccurate, but false. I am sure that others attending the meeting will attest to the fact that I did not say that I would call for a Pittston board meeting to discuss the labor dispute and I did not pledge to resign from the Pittston board if my suggestions were not acted upon. I did say and I did write on stationery provided by the Mayor, a statement which the Mayor felt was acceptable. That statement was (as a director of the Pittston Company I am concerned that a settlement take place which is fair and equitable). I feel that your report is unfair and I feel used. Under the circumstances, I will not meet with you on Monday as planned.

While I personally can tolerate this kind of abuse, I think it unfair that the City Council attempt to attack the Shawmut Bank. Shawmut does not have a banking relationship with the Pittston Company. My involvement with Pittston precedes my association with Shawmut. I hope you will reconsider your proposal to cause harm to a bank which has been such a good corporate citizen for so many years. I will not be making any further statements.

Sincerely,

William F. Craig

cc: Mayor Raymond Flynn
    Mr. Christopher Iannella

An August *Wall Street Journal* Article

An August *Wall Street Journal* article stated that when companies realize that they can save money by negotiating separate contracts with the UMW, they "ask themselves" what is the benefit of the multi-employer bargaining unit. If the BCOA were to fall apart, "you can kiss the UMW goodbye," asserted William Miernyk, a labor economist and long-time observer of the union.

The *Wall Street Journal* article reported that in the green valleys of southwestern Virginia you could tell there was a war on because the only people you saw were in uniform. The men and women on strike from Pittston wore camouflage fatigues and so did their children. The private security men hired by the company wore tight blue jumpsuits and peaked caps. The state troopers dressed like state troopers.

"I'll tell you why these guys wear camouflage," said a local strike supporter as he drove a steady 12 miles an hour past a mine entrance. "First, if you have three or four hundred miners lined up at a mine entrance and maybe a guy chucks a jack-rock in the highway, the state troopers can't tell who from who. Second, you have some concealment in the timber up there." A jack-rock is a rock with three or four three-inch nails bent and welded at the center, like a child's game of jacks only bigger. Unlike a toy jack, it will rip the tire clean off a coal truck; pieces of tire lie in clumps of day lilies at intervals along the mine roads. The other miners' weapons are "rolling blockades" of coal trucks, whose strikers are driving 12 miles an hour along a narrow lane mine road. At the back of the mile-long convoy are four puffing trucks carrying coal. In the deep woods on each side, a flicker of movement betrays a group of miners watching and waiting to rifle bullets into truck windows and tires. Trees have been felled across the road. Scab drivers have been beaten up. Mine supervisors' pickups have been fire bombed. Supervisors responsible for maintaining mine air and water control systems have been beaten, and their homes have been attacked by small arms and vandalism. Coal and violence have been inseparable in the United States. State police reported tire replacement costs of over $500,000 and Pittston costs for tires alone of more than $600,000.

Harassing outside Board members has been a relatively new tactic without recorded success. Most communities and businesses confronted by union character intimidation have ignored the slander.

Union Encourages Bank Account Withdrawal

In October, the seventh month of the strike, Shawmut Bank was getting hit by withdrawals from union investment funds. The AFL-CIO unions drew over 1,000 members to picket outside Shawmut headquarters on the day of the scheduled Shawmut Board of Directors meeting. I was asked by a fellow director if there was anything more I might do to lighten up pressure on the bank.

I responded, "I could quit the Pittston Board or the Shawmut Board. If I left Pittston it would appear that I was pressured to leave and Shawmut would face withdrawal of corporate business by companies upset that the bank would have succumbed to a union strategy that might spread."

The following day, October 18, 1989, a board committee visited my office and asked, "Under what circumstances would you consider leaving Shawmut?"

Having thought about it, I listed terms I considered fair, and I heard the sweet reply, "Anything else?"

The next day there were several headline stories in East Coast newspapers. UMW President Richard Trumka praised Shawmut for reorganizing its social responsibilities, saying, "Craig's retirement should stop Shawmut's massive loss of deposits. Craig, however, said it would be 'disappointing' if his retirement is portrayed as a union victory."

Craig was reported as having said, "It was my decision to leave and not the bank's." He further remarked, "I am aware of the unfair pressure on the bank, and I felt I was the cause of it. Union supporters had demonstrated in the bank's lobby and taken over branches. They blocked the driveway to my home."

Craig praised Secretary of Labor Elizabeth Dole's effort to end the strike by appointing a super mediator, William Usery, a former Secretary of Labor. Usery kept the two sides in meetings for two more months until it became apparent that Pittston could hold out indefinitely with income flowing from non- mining subsidiaries: Brinks and Burlington Northern Airlines (BAX). The Pittston stock price continued to rise despite the strike.

My retirement date was set for December 31, 1989. I was provided with office space, a secretary, a two-year consulting contract and a very adequate lifetime retirement income. Shortly after the announcement of my retirement, Paul O'Brien called, suggesting that he would like to assemble the Business Leaders of Boston in my honor. He suggested having a men's black tie dinner at the Harvard Club in mid November. Paul O'Brien, a golfing buddy and a Concord neighbor, was Chairman and CEO at New York/New England Telephone Co. (NYNX). His company had recently settled a strike with the Electrical Workers Union. NYNX wasn't able to get employees to accept even a modest co-pay for healthcare insurance. We suffered together through neighborhood union car blockades.

Shawmut Chairman, Joel Alvard, thought it was a great idea,

but he insisted that such a tribute should be hosted by Shawmut. A black tie dinner was scheduled for November 21 at the Algonquin Club to celebrate my Boston experience. The invocation was offered by Reverend Monan, President of Boston College. The list of attendees was impressive, and I was overwhelmed by the turnout:

Joel Alvard	Chairman and CEO, Shawmut Bank
Charles Adams	Chairman, Finance Committee, Raytheon Co.
Robert Chandler	President, United Way of Massachusetts Bay
James Cleary	Managing Director, Paine Webber, Inc.
James Crain	VP External Affairs, NE Telephone & Telegraph Co.
John Cullinane	President, Cullinane Group, Inc.
Ralph Dacey	Wellesley, MA
John Driscoll, Esq.	Nutter, McClennen & Fish
Thomas Flatley	President, Flatley Co.
John Foppiano	Price Waterhouse
Walter Gilbert	President, Spaulding/Semoc
William Glavin	President, Babson College
Avram Goldberg	Former Chairman and CEO, The Stop & Shop Cos., Inc.
John Hamill	President, Shawmut Bank
Jack Higgins	Vice President, Kidder, Peabody & Co., Inc.
John Joyce	Vice President and Manager, Alex Brown & Sons, Inc.
John Kaneb	President, Catamount Petroleum Corp.
Joseph Lombard	Salomon Brothers
Norman MacNeil	COO, Ark-Les Corp.
George Macomber	Chairman, George B H Macomber Co.
William McCall	Chairman of the Board, Leggat McCall/ Grubb & Ellis, Inc.
Thomas McDermott	Managing Partner, Ernst & Young
David McGrath, Jr.	President, TAD Technical Services

John McNeice, Jr.	Chairman and CEO, Colonial Management Associates
Harold Miller	President, Houghton Mifflin Co.
Raymond Miller	Consultant, Morgan, Holland Ventures Corp.
Donald Monan, S.J.	President, Boston College
E. James Morton	Chairman and CEO, John Hancock Mutual Life Insurance Co.
Paul Palmer	Vice President and General Manager, IBM
Kevin Phalen	Senior Vice President, Meredith & Grew, Inc.
Edward Phillips	Chairman of the Board, The New England Insurance Co.
L. Guy Reny	President, Standard Duplicator Sales, Inc.
Michael Rushman	President and COO, Cabot, Cabot & Forbes Co.
James Scanlon	Vice President of Marketing, Chicago Title Co.
John Scully	President, John Hancock Mutual Life Insurance Co.
John Shaughnessy, Sr.	President, Shaughnessy Crane Service
Ronald Skates	President and CEO, Data General
Stephen Sweeney	Chairman and CEO, Boston Edison Co.
John Larkin Thompson	President, Blue Cross & Blue Shield of Massachusetts
D. Thomas Trigg	CEO (retired), Shawmut Bank
Vincent Vappi	CEO, Vappi and Co.
Gerald Anderson	President and CEO, Commonwealth Energy System
Joan Bok	Chairman, New England Electric System
Richard Van Pelt	Chairman and CEO, Jordan Marsh
Ned Johnson	CEO, Fidelity Investments
James Coppersmith	Vice President and General Manager, WCVB-TV Channel 5
Philip Haughey	Haughey Co.
Thomas Reilly	Arthur Anderson & Co.
Dave Perini	Perini Corp.

Departing Shawmut Bank was like Jimmy Durante leaving the stage with a series of bows. Shortly after my announced resignation, the Chairman Joel Alvard gathered all the bank officers to a farewell reception at the Harvard Club accompanied by flattering speeches.

W.F. Craig Remarks at the Algonquin Club -11/27/89 Reception and Dinner

I'm complimented, flattered, and honored by the busy people who have gathered to give me a salute here this evening. I believe that everyone at some time in his life has a secret ambition to have a second career and do something different. Most people, however, never have the opportunity. The timing doesn't seem right, or maybe when I'm 60, or maybe I'll get a better offer. For a number of reasons, some more apparent than others, this seems to be the right time for me.

As I look around the room, there are abundant examples of successful career changes:

Bill Glavin –   from Vice Chairman of Xerox to President of
                 Babson College
John Kaneb –   from Chairman of Northeast Petroleum to
                 Owner of Hood Milk
Ron Skates –   from Price Waterhouse Partner to Chairman
                 of Data General

The guy who did the quickest double shift was Jack Driscoll. He went to Dallas eight years ago to invest in real estate, then got smart and returned to Boston as a senior partner of his firm, Nutter, McClennen & Fish. A former partner of that firm, Justice

Louis Brandeis, once remarked that after 55 it would be ideal to begin a new career every five years. He then went on to become a justice of the U. S. Supreme Court, a lifetime appointment.

Some people are so good at redirecting their careers, it's hard to keep track. They don't seem to pause between assignments, like Ray Miller and Jim Scanlon. Yet, there are other leaders who never move; they just change their organizations in a dramatic way, like Tom Flatley, owner of 12 Sheraton Hotels, and Father Donald Monan S. J., President of Boston College.

The culture of an institution reflects the character, ability, and objectives of its leadership. Shawmut has entered a new phase, with new leadership. For those of us who know the team of Alvard, Overstrum and Hamill, we expect a lot. It's an especially balanced combination of experience, youth, and ability. They have an appreciation for the size advantages gained from mergers. I'm sure that when interstate banking gets the green light, Shawmut will be a major national player. I see exciting times ahead, and I'll be in the front row cheering.

If you are fortunate financially to be able to start a second career, the first thing to decide is what it is you want to do. You read so often in the paper that an executive retires early to spend more time with his wife and children. I suggested this to Louise, and she immediately let me know that she already saw enough of me. I insisted that given the opportunity, I could make her a better person.

She replied, "Nevah!"

I've been a banker and lender for 30 years. I'm currently thinking about moving to the investment side of the business, perhaps investment in banks, where the infusion of new management and capital can make a difference.

I hope to continue to serve as an independent outside

director and perhaps add to my directorships. I plan to stay on as Chairman of Massachusetts Higher Education Assistance Corp. and as President of the Boston World Affairs Counsel. I hope to stay active in Boston and look forward to continued association with all of you. I thank Joel, Gunner, and John for this wonderful evening, and I thank you all for coming.

Winners and Losers

The Pittston strike was settled shortly before my Shawmut retirement at the end of 1989. The company did not back down to pressure and remained out of the BCOA. Each Pittston Coal Company employee on January 1 received a $1,000 check for payment of their first 1990 medical bills, pocketing any money not used that year. Any medical cost exceeding $1,000 would be paid 100% by the Pittston Company. Medical insurance cost declined 17%, and the union accepted the existing retirement benefit program. From the UMWA point of view, the disastrous strike didn't gain a thing. The miners, their families, and communities in coal country suffered because of poor union leadership.

I left Shawmut with fond memories at age 58. I was enthusiastic about the future. Richard Trumka went on to become President of the AFL-CIO, his lifetime ambition. How can a society accept outright lies and false accusations in the name of social justice? Who defends community activists who identify wrongdoing in politically favored unions? If it's controversial, don't get involved; go with the flow. Unions once gave strength to the weak, corrected wrongs, and supported the underdog.

Since when should we accept institutional incrimination covered by the public respect for the historic struggle of labor? In my view, the union under Trumka could not hope to bring peace and justice.

I continued as a Pittston board member for another 13 years, when I reached mandatory retirement age of 72 in 2003.

King Coal was getting sidelined, and there was a growing negative national sentiment toward carbon-based energy. New mine permits were delayed by green promoters. International price competition pinched profits. Our production was curtailed by shrinking overseas demand. There was no way our high cost metallurgical coal mines could survive by shifting to delivery of utility fuel.

President Obama initiated directives to suppress coal mining, leading to closed mines and harsh job losses for miners.

West Virginia Senator Jay Rockefeller sponsored a bill that somehow became law. It transferred health and pension benefits for miners of failed companies into an uninsured pool allocated to surviving coal companies.

Pittston Coal Co. was assigned the cost of health and retirement benefits for thousands of miners who never worked for the company. This new burden was worsened by the law's carryover to affiliates. If Pittston Coal was to go under, Brinks and BAX would assume the expense even though the stock of those companies was traded separately. It was Trumka who gave Rockefeller the idea. Government regulation contributed to the coal industry problem, then entered the battlefield shooting the wounded.

Liberty National Golf Club

Metropolitan Petroleum Company was part of Pittston Company when I joined the Board in 1974. The company distributed heating oil in cities along the East Coast from Maryland to New Hampshire, with storage tank farms in Jersey

City, New Haven, and Boston. Metropolitan was frustrated by a long drawn-out effort to build a refinery on the Bay of Fundy in Maine.

The tank farm in Jersey City had first been built by Standard Oil of New Jersey (Esso) in 1907. The property was sold in 1939 to Texaco. Metropolitan acquired the facility in the 1960s and sold it to a British group in 1979.

It was resold again, but as time went on environmental concerns awoke and the EPA inspected sites across the country to identify toxic waste. With over one hundred years of oil storage, the New Jersey property was a standout target in need of correction; enter the lawyers and insurance companies. Responsibility was not in the use but in the language of transfer agreements. The property was sold twice after the Metropolitan sale. The EPA found transfer terms that opted out of environmental responsibility in the most recent transfers. They discovered that Pittston's Metropolitan sale did not include language in the sales agreement absolving the company of any potential toxic claims. The property was put back to Pittston.

Several years went by with claims passing between lawyers and insurance companies until in 2000 when the Pittston president received a visit from the mayor of Jersey City. The mayor did research and met with the EPA and the Corps of Engineers. He proposed a solution for the 100-acre site abutting New York Harbor. The Pittston president, Joe Farrel, presented the mayor's proposal to board. The EPA had estimated a cleanup cost for residential development to be $80,000,000; for commercial restoration, it was estimated to be $36,000,000; and for recreational reuse, the environmental regulators suggested $17,000,000.

Since the cleanup fell back into our laps, we were all for recreation in Jersey City. The mayor specifically identified green open space and suggested we look into building a golf course. Our administration team jumped on it like a fat kid on a Smarty. It was a perfect time for government support. The Corps of Engineers was planning to deepen the New York Harbor nearby, and they assured Pittston that the fill they would supply would be okay with EPA.

Pittston and the Board knew nothing about building golf courses. A deal was made with Tom Kite for a 5% carried interest. Pittston would support his design for a golf course. Donald Trump showed interest, but he was outbid by Paul Fireman, Chairman of Reebok, to complete the development of Liberty National Golf Club. For $20,000,000, Pittston was relieved of the EPA cleanup threat. Pittston directors were looking for a way to exit a potential problem. Paul Fireman undertook a high cost commitment to build a monumental classic use of this New York Harbor scene.

In 2017, the President's Cup was held at the Liberty National Course. I was pleased to see my son Bill, Jr. on TV attending the President's Cup presentation as a guest of the NGA. The next President's Cup matches will be held at his course, the Robert Trent Jones Club on Lake Manassas in Virginia, where son Bill is a club board member.

Pittston had established a mandatory retirement age of 72 for directors. My time was up in 2003. At my final board meeting on May 2, I was asked to serve as Chairman, and the agenda was momentous. The first vote called for the demise of Pittston and Pittston Coal Co. This motion included delisting Pittston from the New York Stock Exchange and replacing it with the Brinks Company. BAX, the heavy freight airline, would report to Brinks. All Pittston Coal Co. property, including mines, gas wells, land, mineral rights, and equipment, would be sold to form a VIBA fund dedicated to meet all legal obligations, including healthcare and retirement obligations. There was little debt to be paid, and the actuarially calculated VIBA need was $1 billion, an amount covered by audited asset value of the property to be liquidated, including over forty operating mines, 100,000 acres of land and mineral rights, forests with timber mills, and two natural gas producing fields. Purchasers of the mines and equipment would continue operating properties with economic life, retaining associated miners. Time will tell, but there were no losers. Alan Greenspan might call it 'Destructive Innovation.'

Pittston shares were converted to Brinks. Having served as a director for 30 years, I had accumulated a fair share of options and stock and was pleased to see that shareholders did not suffer; to the contrary, they gained from the coal business exit.

The completed agenda was anticipated by the Board, having studied our options at previous meetings. The motions were passed, and I gaveled the end of the meeting and the passing of my long and exciting Pittston experience. The meeting was followed by a reception with senior management, undeserved warm speeches about my departure, and remembrance tokens. I felt like someone was saying, "And please turn out the lights as you close the door."

INVENTING ONESELF

WHAT'S NEXT?

Upon leaving Shawmut in 1989 at the age of 58, I had no interest in retirement; even with future financial needs fully covered, I really believed what I said about seeking an independent new career. There were flattering job offers, but I was eager to form my own business. Shawmut Chairman Joel Alvard, with Board approval, offered me the use of the Provident Bank executive suite on Winter Street in downtown Boston. The Provident was owned by Hartford National prior to the merger with Shawmut, and Joel used the space as his headquarters. The layout of this stone building included several furnished rooms: a paneled multi-windowed office with working fireplace, a conference room, secretary's room, library, dining room, kitchen, and bath. These rooms were part of a mansion that fronted on Temple Street. It was built in 1840 by the owner of a whale oil company. Added to this original house was a high-rise modern glass bank building with the Winter Street address.

I spent the next year considering investment opportunities. The process followed the path most investors seek to track. Look for high yield, low risk in a field they understand. In my case, it was clearly banking. Fred Kirby helped me come to that conclusion. He was disappointed that I chose to leave Shawmut Bank, but as a fellow Pittston director he understood and felt I made the right decision. He sent me a letter suggesting that if I could find a modestly mismanaged company to acquire, he would assist financially with the purchase. A week later, a follow-up letter arrived reassuring me of his commitment but adding his encouragement to seek to buy a business that I understood. Since he was chairman and majority shareholder in Investor's Diversified Services (IDS), he indicated that acquiring a mutual fund management company might be the way to go. He even had a suggestion in the Boston area; however, I felt even more confident that I should stick with banking.

The New York Times / Larry C. Morris

Photo of Fred Kirby.

17 DeHart St., P.O. Box 151, Morristown, N.J. 07960-0151
201-538-4800   212-732-2265

September 13, 1988

MEMORANDUM

To: Bill Craig

From: F. M. Kirby

Subj: Our private discussion of September 9th

     After our talk, and because you referred to the possibility of entering a field other than banking, and because you said you might like to be "the head man" in your next and final career vehicle, and because you in-dicated an interest in investing some of your substantial net worth in such vehicle, it occurred to me that you might like to go into the investment management business either alone, with Alleghany or with me as a fairly silent partner.

     Herewith are copies of some correspondence which happens to be going over my desk at the present time on this subject. I am in no way recommending this particular investment manage-ment company but, if it should interest you, please feel free to contact Mr. Leeson.

Fred

FMK:msw

Enclosures

Bank Investing

I looked at bank investments around the country and concluded:

(1) Bank accounting couldn't be trusted

(2) Asset values were often overstated

(3) Earnings were erratic

(4) Most areas were over-banked, providing low margins

(5) There was little upside to buying stock in a conservatively managed bank. You would be resisted as an outsider, and one might question available information

(6) Since government makes the rules, they should be the only partners to be trusted

In 1990, distressed banks, burdened by a high percentage of nonperforming real estate loans, had their capital accounts ground down to negative worth by write-offs. Regulators recognized investor and management failure and sought a resolution.

The Federal Deposit Insurance Corporation (FDIC) arrested depositor concerns; however, the FDIC did not aim to put these mismanaged banks back on their feet. Their practice was to negate the failed bank's license and transfer banking authorization to a well-capitalized stable institution.

The government (the FDIC is part of the US Treasury Department) assumed the cost of restructuring so that branches could be consolidated and new investors indemnified against former shareholder, lessor, vendor, customer, borrower, or employee litigation. The FDIC provided a trapdoor into which problem loans, not identified at the time the bank changed hands, could for three years be transferred back to the FDIC. Most deals involved sound banks taking over weak ones: Fleet, NCNB, Bank One, and Core States. There were no non-bank investment groups. Closer observation showed that subsequent to takeover, the combined bank posted higher performance, mainly due to acquiring the government supported restructured bank.

I observed how much more attractive it would be for private investment to go directly to the restructuring rather than seeking the benefit through investment in another bank, (i.e., buy shares in Fleet Bank to take advantage of a restructured Bank of New England).

It would be a chance to buy assured quality and a high return on equity without paying a premium. It would be a one-time opportunity to wash out high cost, less dependable money, borrowed and brokered funds, shake down operating expenses, pick and choose earning assets to be retained, and convert high risk loans to investment quality assets. A bonus feature would be the elimination of high cost back office redundancy – EDP and systems inefficiencies — by outsourcing such services.

My interests, and the same for other investors, would be to maintain high liquidity, low cost, low risk, and sell out within three years. Directors would be required to have at least $1 million invested in the company's common stock, and they would be ineligible to borrow from the new bank.

Forming a Plan

In May 1990, I spoke with John LaWare, Federal Reserve Board Governor. He had been Chairman at Shawmut Bank when I was President. I told him about my plan and asked for an introduction to the FDIC. He called back, having contacted William Seidman, Chairman of the FDIC. The message was that I should call Harrison Young, who headed the department dealing with failed banks. He was the chief negotiator in the Bank of New England takeover by Fleet Bank with KKR financing.

John added, "When you make an appointment, plan to stay overnight at my house and bring Louise."

When I visited Mr. Young a week later, he wanted to know my source of capital. I listed several wealthy investors who would be willing to join my group. If more capital were needed, I planned to engage an investment banking firm to fill out any shortage. I did not anticipate any borrowing; I planned to use private equity. This was before the term became popular. I mentioned that I was authorized by Massachusetts to form an investment company named "Charter Capital Corp." As President, my offices were in the Provident Bank building at 20 Winter Street in Boston. Traditionally, the FDIC would protect the depositors of such failed banks by arranging a merger with a larger secure regional bank; however, in 1990, most larger banks were on a Federal Reserve watch list, singled out as being inadequately capitalized as the result of growing nonperforming and criticized loans. My plan, at the time, was to invest and raise capital from other private investors to purchase foreclosed banks. At the Washington, D.C. headquarters of the FDIC, I explained my plan to use personal savings and non-debt commitments and use an investment bank under contract to raise any additional funds needed beyond personal relationships.

After detailed evaluation by Harrison Young, Managing Director of the FDIC Department for Foreclosure Resolution, Chairman William Seidman agreed that his office would welcome a bid by the group I would form. Individual investors had never before been cleared to bid against selected banks.

WILLIAM F. CRAIG

JOHN P. LAWARE

November 9, 1989

Mr. William F. Craig
Vice Chairman
Shawmut Bank, N.A.
One Federal Street
Boston, Massachusetts 02211

Dear Bill:

First, I wish I could be with your many other
friends this evening to wish you well as you leave
after a very distinguished tour of duty. I say that
from deep personal conviction and ten years of
experience. Your firm hand on the credit tiller
guided the Shawmut sloop through some pretty rocky
waters with hardly a scratch. There are so many
instances of your wisdom and keen market judgments
keeping us out of trouble. Need I even mention
Brazil? In addition, you were always the most
popular member of the senior management team with
customers -- except, of course, when you took their
money on the golf course.

Bill, I have missed you from a personal as
well as professional point of view since I shifted
down here 15 months ago, and I know that the bank
and your associates will sorely miss your counsel
as the New England region goes into another period
of trial. But, I am sure they share my affection
and good will for you and Louise and your wonderful
family and join in wishing you many years of happiness,
fruitful activity and good health in the future.

Sincerely,

John P. LaWare

197

WILLIAM F. CRAIG

30 WINTER STREET
BOSTON, MA 02108
(617) 423-5091

153 GARFIELD ROAD
CONCORD, MA 01742
(508) 369-5188

November 13, 1989

Honorable John P. LaWare
Governor
Federal Reserve Board
B2064 Federal Reserve Building
20th & Constitution Avenue, NW
Washington, DC 20551

Dear John:

You were thoughtful to write in connection with my retirement from Shawmut. Your comments were very touching and I appreciate receiving the good wishes you expressed. While the term retirement is used officially, I certainly have no plans to sit back and do nothing. My plans were to leave Shawmut next year some time, but the United Mine Workers strike pressure hastened my departure. It came down to either leaving the Pittston Board or the Shawmut and I felt it would be a very bad precedent for me to give in to intimidation. The union was very effective in influencing the withdrawal of funds from the bank. So, I arranged to leave a little earlier than I might otherwise have done. For the next few weeks I will be talking with people about the possibility of putting together an investment company specializing in acquiring banks. I have been encouraged to do this by two or three substantial investors. I know others have been active along these lines. I don't plan to dive ahead without one or two other people who can bring something to the party. After some discussion, I may find it better to turn in an entirely difference direction. Only time will tell.

Everyone at the Shawmut has been very gracious and supportive about my taking leave. I have always hoped that circumstances would permit me to enjoy a second career. I think the time to move on is when things are going well, when one's health is good, and when there are enough years to see not only the beginning of a new career, but some fruits resulting from the effort. My career to date has been most rewarding and much of that satisfaction results from the people I have had the good fortune to associate with. I dearly enjoyed the time we shared together and reflect on the many benefits that came from my association with you. Thank you for all you have done in the past and for your kind encouragement as I make this move.

Sincerely,

Bill

Gaining Acceptance

I engaged Nutter, McClennen & Fish as counsel and Price Waterhouse as our accountants. Harrison stated that the FDIC insisted that they reserve discussions to qualified banks and private investors. Sharing documents and authorizing onsite inspections and other due diligence activity must be limited to real potential buyers. He noted that many banks were operating under Federal Reserve Bank cease and desist letters, limiting expansion due to inadequate reserves and heavy loan write-offs.

"We don't want to be accused of leaning one drunk against another," Harrison said. "That gives us more willingness to encourage qualified investors to work with us. Bill, you qualify from what you have told me. We'll check out your story."

Chairman Seidman concluded that my background assured him that I might be able to pull it off. The FDIC knew I was without deep pockets, but after checking out my background and where my support was coming from, I got the go ahead.

I told Harrison that after attending several investor information meetings, which were basically policy discussions, I concluded that the time available between problem bank announcements, information meetings, bid meetings, bid acceptance, and official closing was insufficient to do analysis, due diligence, legal work, bid structuring, and raising the money. He agreed, realizing that a private investor lacked what big banks brought to the table, namely, large staffs of accountants and in-house lawyers who could assign large groups of executives to accelerate the process. I explained that as an individual investor I could duplicate the needed path followed by big bank bid competitors, but to do so I would need to have outside legal and accounting talent, assuming hundreds of thousands of expense dollars to prepare a bid, not knowing it would be a winning bid.

Mr. Young recognized the disadvantage a private investor with limited staff would have bidding against big banks.

"Bill, you mentioned looking into the possibility of bidding for a distressed bank in the northeast states," Young said. "Focus on New Hampshire. There are five banks in the state with negative net worth. We'll share some already public information with you. Pick one and see what you can do."

In June I went hunting for the right investment banker. I talked with friends at Merrill Lynch, First Boston, and Lehman Bros. Gerry McGinley and Bob Goldhammer in the New York office and Jack Higgins in the Boston office at Kidder Peabody introduced me to their chief merger and acquisitions officer in the New York office, Marshall Davidson. Marshall had the right kind of experience, the respect of regulation, and was enthusiastic about the idea. Before getting Kidder Peabody to sign on, I visited privately at lunch or dinner with the CEO of each of the five banks mentioned by Harrison Young as in need of refinancing. Each of them held out hope the FDIC would provide open assistance and keep them alive.

Bob Keller at Dartmouth Bank had serious doubts they could pull it off. Dartmouth Bank had a loss in 1989 of $42.4 million and in 1990 of $85 million. In two years the bank suffered losses of over $127 million, wiping out the capital account of the bank.

I told Bob Keller that I planned to hire Davidson from Kidder Peabody to seek investment opportunities in the troubled bank area, and I suggested meeting with the Dartmouth Bank Board to see if there might be a solution to their problem.

Bob arranged a special board meeting, which Davidson and I attended. Keller convinced the Board to sign a consulting contract with Kidder Peabody. After a few weeks, Davidson convinced Keller and his Board that it was unlikely that the FDIC would keep them open. I told Keller that it was likely that all five troubled New Hampshire banks would be closed by the FDIC and reopened with financing from winning bids. Bob Keller joined Dartmouth Bank in 1990 and was made CEO later that year. He was with the Fleet-owned Indian Head Bank of New Hampshire for 13 years, where he was EVP, CFO, and Chief Administrative Officer. Mr. Keller gained extensive experience in consolidating bank operations while serving at American Federal Bank in Dallas, which was created through the merger of 12 independent thrifts. He supervised the closing of over 40 branches and the conversion of three data processing systems. He earned his CPA while at Arthur Anderson prior to his banking career.

Failed Banks and the New Hampshire Presidential Primary

If you looked at the books of any New Hampshire bank, you saw a common story reflecting the boom and bust of the state's economy. In 1991, politicians were trudging around the state preparing for the upcoming presidential primary. It was where the candidates would get their first feel for the mood of the country. They would hear tales of unprecedented gloom and economic woe, where four years before there was speculative frenzy. One is explained by the other. In the mid '80s, especially in the ski and lake areas, roads were lined with planned resort communities, mostly empty. In Woodstock, a few miles from Loon Mountain, a local real estate agent said that a condo that might have sold for $150,000 three years ago would now sell (if he could find a buyer) for about $75,000. And throughout the state, agents couldn't give commercial property away. Many builders with construction loans from New Hampshire banks just threw in the keys to foreclosed property and left the banks with the write-off problem. In 1988, unemployment statewide was 3½%;

in 1991 it was over 7%. President George Bush was coming to New Hampshire to drum up support for his second term primary election. Banks were more concerned about collecting overdue loans than seeking new loan business. Residents of the state were aware that half of their deposits were in banks with empty capital accounts. The pressure was on Washington to take action, and the Administration didn't want President Bush traveling throughout the state without an answer to the problem.

The FDIC, part of the US Treasury Department, realized that they had limited time to do the job. In a meeting with Governor Judd Gregg (Republican), Mr. Seidman (FDIC Chairman) made it clear that government assistance would be forthcoming only in partnership with private capital infusion into struggling banks.

At my request, John Fopiano, a Price Waterhouse Boston partner, requested from Price Waterhouse's Washington office, research information about every FDIC assisted transaction for the past three years. There were no investor groups, just banks refinancing failed banks.

We wished to take advantage of precedent and collated into our draft proposal items favorable to our investors. This became the outline for our proposed bid. At a meeting at my office, which included John Foppiano, Price Waterhouse; Mike Krebs, Nutter, McClennen & Fish; and Marshall Davidson, Kidder Peabody, the outline of a proposal was designed.

Today

★★★

No free ride for N.H. banks

45 The Federal Deposit Insurance Corp. tells N.H. Gov. Judd Gregg that government assistance for struggling banks will be forthcoming only in partnership with private capital infusions.

2-5-91

THE BOSTON GLOBE • TU

FDIC expects private funds to help N.H. banks

By Mitchell Zuckoff
GLOBE STAFF

Federal Deposit Insurance Corp. chairman L. William Seidman yesterday strengthened his commitment to treat New Hampshire as "an experiment" in ways to aid rather than close ailing banks.

But in a meeting with New Hampshire Gov. Judd Gregg, Seidman made it clear that government assistance will be forthcoming only in partnership with private capital infusions into struggling banks.

That could prove to be a deal-killer for some New Hampshire banks, several of which are considered too unstable to attract significant outside investments, analysts and bankers said.

"Any bank in New England that has gone looking for capital, in light of our economic situation, has found it simply unavailable," said Christopher C. Gallagher, legislative counsel for the New Hampshire Bankers' Association.

Seidman met in Washington with Gregg, who is leading an effort to prevent the collapse of New Hampshire banks under the weight of bad real estate debt. Gregg hopes Seidman, the nation's top bank regulator, will consider the state's largest banks as collectively "too big to fail"

and, therefore, eligible for aggressive federal action.

"He was very enthusiastic about using New Hampshire as, in his words, an experiment," Gregg said in a telephone interview. "He is giving us a very bright green light to come up with some initiatives. He sees New Hampshire as a good place to try approaches that haven't been tried to date."

Gregg said he and Seidman did not discuss individual banks or specific plans; that, the governor said, is the job of the banks themselves in the weeks ahead. One scenario considered likely is the consolidation of two or more troubled banks as a way to reduce operating costs and convince the FDIC that they are serious about slimming down to survive.

Although Gregg said he was encouraged by Seidman's willingness to be flexible, the governor acknowledged that the mandate for private funds could prove troublesome.

"It is a major hurdle, but it's not unreasonable to expect that the FDIC would want to see some private participation before it put in public dollars in a nonclosure situation," Gregg said. "That's the challenge, and it's one which some imaginative people can meet."

Ralph Jensen, chief executive of Numerica Savings Bank in Manches-

L. WILLIAM SEIDMAN

ter, said it is possible that Seidman's commitment to provide assistance to open banks could pry loose capital from otherwise wary investors. He added, however, that it is too early to tell how Seidman's comments will be received.

"We'll never know until we get the checks," Jensen said.

Gallagher said he remained hopeful that Seidman could be persuaded to treat savings from consolidation as, in effect, outside capital. The alternative, Gallagher said, might be picking up the tab for bank closures.

Asked whether that was a halfway solution that would not demonstrate the banks' future solvency, Gallagher said: "Half a loaf? Maybe. It's still bread, whether it's wheat bread or white bread."

The FDIC discouraged pursuing a single bank acquisition, suggesting we go for two troubled banks. After detailed analysis of the other 4 banks, we decided to combine our bid for Dartmouth Bank with Numeria. It was estimated that such an increased equity capital requirement would total $70 million. Harrison Young suggested that the government was prepared to provide $20 million in the form of a preferred stock purchase, provided my group raised $50 million.

Recognizing the improved earning capability resulting from a two-bank merger— through improved efficiency, and reduced overhead costs, through branch office closings, and a combined back office expense reduction— we would have a better story to tell, making it likely for us to raise the additional $10 million.

I planned to invest $1.5 million, and I knew I could count on $2 million from Fred Kirby. I had an indication of interest from John J. Byrne, Chairman of Fund America Co. who lived in Hanover, New Hampshire, for $7 million. Fred had recently sold Investor Diversified Services (IDS) to American Express, while John Byrne sold Travelers Insurance Co. to American Express. They took stock amounting to about 20% of the company ownership and they both were American Express directors. Charles Hugel, who lived in New Hampshire, could be counted on for $2 million. The former Chairman of RJR Nabisco and Combustion Engineering succeeded Fred Kirby as Chairman of Lafayette College, and preceded Jeff Kirby in that position. Jeff would be in for $1 million. Add to the impressive list of investors: Edward A Fox, the Dean of the Amos Tuck School of Business Administration at Dartmouth College and the former President and CEO (from 1973 to 1990) of the Student Loan Marketing Association (Sallie Mae). I knew him from my days as Chairman of the Massachusetts Higher Education Assistance Corp. The

New Hampshire Retirement System indicated that they were interested in investing $4 million. (I might add that William Seidman graduated from Dartmouth College.)

Re-enter the Browning Connection

This being the first time the FDIC would ask for bids for more than one bank serving the same market appealed to investors, as any potential investor's first question was: "Who's in the deal?" The list of likely investors mentioned above totaled $23 million. It should be a meaningful inducement for Kidder Peabody to bring in the additional $27 million.

One of my most interesting investor solicitation visits was at the Sky Club in New York City with John Burns, President of Allegheny Corp., who had circled $2 million of the new Dartmouth Bank offering. John mentioned that George McFadden was a good friend of Fred Kirby's and that McFadden Brothers had joined in several Allegheny investments. John offered George enthusiastic support for my deal. I knew that George McFadden had some affection for New Hampshire since he graduated from Saint Paul's Academy in Concord, New Hampshire. I didn't mention that my father was chauffeur for his aunt, Mrs. Browning, and I grew up with his cousins, Bobby and Mickey McFadden, during summers in Bar Harbor.

John and George joined me for lunch at the University Club in New York. A month later, McFadden wrote back thanking me for my time, material and presentation, but said, "I think it's a little too cold in New Hampshire for my taste."

No comment from me.

I would have been interested in his reaction if I told him that my father died of heart failure in 1964 at the age of 68, and that my mother received my dad's monthly salary until Mrs. Browning died in 1979. Payments were made from a McFadden Bros. Trust for 14 years. When Mrs. Browning died, her will provided Mom with a lifetime income from a $2 million trust account set up at Gerard Trust in Philadelphia. When my mother died, the principal was divided between the Bar Harbor Hospital and the Seacoast Missions. To protect the principal's residuum, funds were invested by the Trust company in US Government bonds. Mother died at age 94. For 15 years she collected on average $125,000 each year. During that period, government bond rates ran between 5% and 7%.

My mother never worked for Mrs. Browning, but after my father died, once a month Mom would visit Mrs. Browning in her Philadelphia mid-city apartment on Rittenhouse Square or at the Barclay Hotel across the street for lunch. Mrs. Browning was fond of my mother and obviously felt the same way about my dad. Mom would often bring rice pudding with raisins and real cream or a baked Irish scone. She was frequently criticized by my brothers, Dennis and Jack, that she showed favoritism for son Bill and Mrs. Browning because we always got more raisins than they did. When our mother died, she left Dennis, Jack, and me $200,000 each. I don't know what they did with the money, but I paid off the mortgage I had on our summer house in Eagles Mere.

Too bad George McFadden didn't participate by investing in New Dartmouth Bank. He would have returned to the McFadden estate much more than the Craigs received. God bless Mrs. Browning. She certainly gave my immigrant family a leg up in this world.

Structuring the Deal

In May 1991, I visited with Harrison Young at the FDIC office in Washington. He mentioned that the FDIC would like to receive conforming bids for three banks rather than two, adding the New Hampshire Savings Bank in Concord, New Hampshire, with over $900 million in deposits. The minimum bid would remain the same, $70 million, but the structure of the bid would be made more appealing to investors by increasing the non-voting preferred stock to be purchased from the winning bidder to $30 million from the $20 million previously agreed. It would not require the investors to increase their common stock target of $40 million.

Young said the three banks New Dartmouth sought to acquire were savings banks. The other distressed New Hampshire banks were commercial national banks under control of the Comptrollers Office and should be bid separately. This was good news for two reasons. First, it indicated that the pool of potential bidders was not deep, and when we got closer to the Presidential Primary date, the pressure was on to bring about a solution for the insolvent New Hampshire banks.

Newspapers reported that confidential sources identified six bank bidders: Fleet/Norstar, Providence; Key Corp., Albany; First New Hampshire Banks, which is owned by the Bank of Ireland; the Craig Group; Harvard Management Co., caretakers of Harvard University's $10 billion endowment; and John Hancock Insurance Co.

I wasn't that concerned about the three commercial banks mentioned, but I was upset to learn about Harvard and Hancock since I had met with their senior staff, discussed our strategy and offered them the opportunity to participate with my group. The material they were given required confidentiality.

Bob Stone, a fellow Pittston director and good friend, was one of five Harvard University governors and overseer of the endowment fund. I spoke with Bob in New York City after a Pittston board meeting. He said, "Don't worry about Harvard."

After a Saturday evening Mass at my church, (Saint Bernard in Concord, Massachusetts), I spoke with John McGee, a John Hancock Life Insurance Co. director, informing him about my visit with his VP of Finance, giving him the total story, sharing confidential information, soliciting Hancock participation, offering the Craig Group bid plan, and the fact that I had read in the paper that Hancock may be planning to submit their own bid. "It doesn't seem right, John. Please check it out and call me."

The next Monday, McGee called with the message, "Don't worry about Hancock."

The speculation, repeated in several newspapers about potential bidders, included articles in the *Wall Street Journal, New York Times, American Banker,* and *Boston Globe,* caused me to worry. Most expressed doubt that a single investor could come up with $70 million. I realized that if I failed, I would be responsible to pay the fees generated by my legal and accounting support. I had the full-time commitment of Mike Krebs from Nutter, McClennen & Fish at $300 an hour. Jack Driscoll, the senior partner, kept me posted on the estimated bill.

As of August 1991, my legal bill for Nutter, McClennen & Fish was estimated to be $400,000, and Price Waterhouse estimated my accounting fees would exceed $375,000. These costs would come out of my pocket if my bid failed. Pledged participants assumed no obligation if my deal fell through.

Kidder Peabody filtered back to me concerns of a few of the larger participants of my group. Now that it began to appear that we could win the bid, the thought was that while I was to get

$1 million of common stock and warrants to purchase at the original offering price, a sufficient number of shares to bring my position up to 10% of outstanding common stock caused other investors to be concerned about the dilution it would cause.

My response was, "Who else was willing to spend a year bringing it all together? And who among the investors was willing to assume the cost of needed accounting and legal expenses, which when combined with putting my reputation on the line, gave the Craig Group creditability? No warrants, no deal." Kidder Peabody's Marshall Davidson passed back the word and the protests were dropped.

Legal and Accounting Advice

In mid-July, Price Waterhouse reported on their extensive due diligence efforts (3,200 billable hours). Their team of 10 CPAs spent two weeks probing the three distressed banks. Their analysis included 42 pages of comments and suggestions. A condensed summary included:

(1) All three banks are not in compliance with minimum regulatory capital guidelines and are failing due to problem real estate loans.

(2) In order to preserve the remaining capital, it appears that the loan charge-offs are not being recorded in a timely way.

(3) The review disclosed that loans were not properly rated. Of 61 loans reviewed, 33 should have been downgraded for documentation deficiencies. This would indicate that there were additional loans at each of the banks, which should be classified and therefore put into the Segregated Asset Pool (SAP). The SAP within New Dartmouth Bank

would house nonperforming and classified assets of the troubled institutions. Assistance on the SAP by the FDIC would cause the pool to be earnings-neutral to New Dartmouth Bank and ultimately turned over to the FDIC Bank. Premises, including redundant branch buildings and head offices, as well as equipment, leasehold improvements, etc., not utilized by New Dartmouth Bank would be placed in the SAP under the same terms as other segregated assets.

(4) A large portion of the residential loan portfolio of each of the banks consists of "nonconforming" loans, i.e., loans that have nonstandard or missing documentation. Such loans are highly illiquid and accordingly could require significant discounts in order to sell.

(5) Two of the banks, Dartmouth and New Hampshire Savings Banks, have home equity loans that call for balloon payments at the end of either five or ten years. Prior to the balloon payment, these loans require that only interest be paid. Many of these loans were made from 1986 to 1988 when New Hampshire real estate was at its peak. If borrowers sell or abandon their homes prior to maturity of the loans, there may not be sufficient equity to repay outstanding balances.

(6) New Hampshire Savings Bank had sold approximately $219 million residential mortgage loans with recourse. The FDIC agreement does not cover the risk of recourse.

(7) Information with respect to the bank's operations, EDP, accounting and operating procedures were evaluated, and recommendations were provided.

At about the same time:

(1) The Nutter, McClennen & Fish report included reviewing and commenting on the FDIC bid materials.

(2) Performed limited due diligence regarding general corporate and real estate matters of the target institutions in concert with our other advisors.

(3) Advised us on the optimal regulatory structure for New Dartmouth Bank.

(4) Assisted us in preparing and prosecuting the requisite regulatory applications.

(5) Drafted portions and reviewed private placement memorandum.

(6) Reviewed investor subscription materials.

(7) Drafted and/or reviewed, as appropriate, all necessary corporate charter documents, executive employment agreements, employee stock plans and various closing papers.

On August 18 a meeting was held in Washington with:

FDIC	Harrison Young
	Gail Patelunas
	Leslie Schafer (legal staff)
	David Massey (outside counsel)
Craig Group	Bill Craig – Charter Capital Corp.
	Marshall Davidson – Kidder Peabody
	Mike Krebs – Nutter, McClennen & Fish
	Russell Kemp – Evaluation Associates
	(advisor to New Hampshire Pension System)

The meeting was held in response to a letter I had written to Harrison Young offering suggestions and requesting assistance regarding specific weaknesses exposed through our combined due diligence efforts. Leslie Schafer started the session stating a few obvious facts: There would be two separate bids, one for the two commercial national banks (Amoskeg and Bank East) and another separate bid for a combination of the three savings banks (Dartmouth, Numeria and New Hampshire Savings Bank.) The troubled banks would be placed in receivership prior to the closing of the transaction in order to most fully protect the FDIC's interest with respect to undisclosed liabilities, such as successfully prosecuting lender liability suits against the troubled institutions. Also in this manner the new investors would be protected most fully against such contingent liabilities.

In essence, the merger would represent a "closed bank" assistance transaction. Troubled assets would be written down to approximate fair value and carried on the books of New Dartmouth Bank at those values within a Segregated Asset Pool (SAP). The three New Hampshire banks would be combined into a $3 billion entity with significant operating economies resulting from branch consolidation, data processing out-placement, staff reduction, pension and healthcare previous obligations, etc., resulting in non-interest expenses to average assets at .03% or less, offering a likely return on investment of 20%.

The acquisition of New Dartmouth Bank by new investors, including Craig, the lead investor responsible for overall management of New Dartmouth Bank, would take place as a taxable purchase; (i.e., assets and liabilities of the troubled institutions would be market-to-market for both financial reporting and tax purposes).

It all sounds very formal, but again it's all plus-plus. The only liabilities we purchase are deposits, the source funding our assets, and the only assets we purchase are earning assets with limited risk because, over the three following years, any purchased assets could be put back to the government if threatened by a possible loss of income.

We proceeded to discuss our due diligence discovery and there was agreement to cover our concerns.

Harrison said the FDIC had been discussing with the Department of Justice (DOJ) their concern regarding seeking bids to combine three banks. The DOJ was "going crazy" trying to grapple with the antitrust issues implicated by the FDIC packaging. FDIC staff was scheduled to meet with DOJ staff that day. Young indicated that he would not be willing to circumvent DOJ on antitrust concerns.

We discussed the convertibility of preferred stock and the warrants to purchase common stock after three years. Craig suggested that NDB would be willing to structure a non-convertibility feature so as to impose penalties upon the bank for failure to redeem as scheduled, and that warrants should be cancellable pro rata for the early redemption of preferred stock.

Young responded rather obliquely that the warrant terms were designed to achieve a certain result, although he could not at that instant recall the reasoning. He implied that if the preferred stock were redeemed within three years, the warrants would be withdrawn. Young indicated that the FDIC would prefer not to have any equity interest. Capitalization of New Dartmouth Bank would be provided initially by the new investors and the FDIC. Eventually New Dartmouth should be 100% privately held. As a general proposition, the FDIC would be looking to reduce its equity interest.

Patelunas said that the FDIC reviewed our comments regarding Price Waterhouse's analysis of the distressed banks. Corrections would be made before the asset transfers.

213

Craig and Davidson reviewed at some length Keller's experience and his role and strengths that helped in attracting capital. Young emphasized that Keller could not accompany Craig's team to meetings with the FDIC. "Keller is effectively working for the FDIC and in theory should be available to respond to inquiries from all interested bidders." Familiar with Keller and the history of Craig's involvement with Dartmouth, "If we (the Division for Restructuring of Failed Banks) thought Keller had a black spot on his forehead, we would have told you that Keller had a black spot on his forehead." He also noted the need to submit management's plan as part of the chartering process. FDIC must review Keller's status with other regulators and cannot make a decision on any individual until after a bid is submitted.

Patelunas added: FDIC wants to avoid appearance that senior management of any failed bank is "in the pocket" of any particular investor, because that may lead other potential investors to believe that they will not have the same access to information about that bank and consequently diminish the pool of interested bidders.

The Winning Bid

Young anticipated a closing between mid September and early October. The Charter Capital Corp. Craig Group bid was submitted on my birthday, September 16, 1991. The FDIC, in a news release on October 10, 1991, announced: Three savings banks in New Hampshire were closed today and will be reopened Friday as branches of New Dartmouth Bank, a newly chartered bank to be headquartered in Manchester, New Hampshire. They are the $917 million-deposit New Hampshire Savings Bank, Concord; the $818 million-deposit Numeria Savings Bank,

Manchester, and New Dartmouth Bank, which is owned by an investor group led by William F. Craig, Boston, a former President of Shawmut and Vice Chairman of Shawmut Corporation. The estimated government cost of the three savings bank failures is approximately $624 million.

The two failed New Hampshire commercial banks – Amoskeg Bank and Bank East with combined deposits of $1.1 billion – will become part of First New Hampshire Bank, a subsidiary of Bank of Ireland First Holdings, a US subsidiary of Bank of Ireland, Dublin.

FDIC Chairman William Seidman said: "We are announcing an infusion of public and private sector funds that will result in a New Hampshire banking system better positioned to meet needs of the area's businesses and consumers and better able to weather future economic storms."

The transactions announced were unusual for several reasons. One is that instead of marketing the failed banks individually to potential purchasers, the FDIC this time packaged the three savings banks into a single franchise for sale. Other noteworthy elements of the transaction included: A "shared equity" feature whereby the FDIC will temporarily infuse cash into New Dartmouth Bank by agreeing to purchase perpetual preferred stock on a short-term basis. This feature is designed to help the acquiring institution obtain the capital needed to complete the transaction but on terms favorable enough to the FDIC that the bank will want to redeem the preferred stock quickly.

Under the transaction with New Dartmouth Bank, the FDIC will purchase $31.5 million of the non-voting preferred stock in the bank. That represents about 45% of the new bank's initial capital, with the rest coming from the investor group headed by Mr. Craig. The stock may be redeemed at any time under a formula that increases over time. The redemption price formula is intended partly to minimize the bank's financing burden in the early years, while giving the private investor group strong incentives to redeem the FDIC's shares as soon as possible.

The news was released at a reception at the New Hampshire Governor's Office, attended by Governor Gregg, Bill Seidman, Harrison Young, the State Banking Commissioner, a few state senators, TV personalities with their cameras, and the press. Everyone had something nice to say, including Bill Marshall, President of First New Hampshire Bank. Bill had only recently been hired by the Bank of Ireland, Dublin, to oversee their New Hampshire subsidiary, which had experienced significant losses for the past few years. He had been with me at Shawmut for about 10 years. I remember asking him to move from Boston to Springfield, Massachusetts, as President of the Shawmut Bank of Springfield. He loved the move.

William F. Craig responding on TV to the announcement of the winning bid for the three banks at the New Hampshire Governor's Office. With Governor Gregg, Harrison Young and Bill Marshall.

Everything went as planned at New Dartmouth Bank, and after a few weeks of operations I realized that unless I moved to Manchester, New Hampshire, from Concord, Massachusetts, I could not fill the job as CEO. Closing branches, ending leases, negotiating electronic systems outsourcing, and delegating senior management authority required on-site presence. The Board of Directors agreed that I should continue to fill the role of lead investor and Chairman of the Board overseeing management, with full support of the Board. There would be no change in my $250,000 compensation or my employment agreement to have the right to exercise warrants to purchase additional shares of common stock at the original offering price, to bring my stock ownership up to a 10% owner of New Dartmouth Bank. I knew that as president, Bob Keller had his people in place and would need little overseeing. It was a drag to drive 35 miles each day to Manchester when once a week could cover my reduced role.

The NDB proceeded as planned. The bank was making $2 million a month after tax and within two years we paid off the perpetual preferred, thereby eliminating the warrants that threatened serious dilution.

Reaping the Reward

The three-year period we were allowed to put back to the government's Segregated Asset Pool (SAP) any classified or underperforming loan would be running out in one year. Our plan from the beginning was to sell out within three years. Arrangements were made for three investment banks to suggest how to find the right buyer. We selected Goldman Sachs. They knew NDB would be attractive to a large bank. The bank had no loan problems due to the three-year putback clause. The recent consolidation of branches gave the bank low funding costs, and

CitiBank was contracted to administer all back office services. With net income running at the $20 million level, an eight times earnings was justified.

My friends at Shawmut were happy to take the deal and offered a nontaxable stock for stock purchase totaling $160,000,000. My share was $16,000,000 less ordinary income tax on exercised warrants and capital gains tax on appreciated value. The capital gains tax was delayed since the sale was in the form of a tax-free exchange of stock. Having been the first private investor to submit a winning bid to acquire failed banks from the government, I was curious to observe whether the path I ventured on would be followed by future investment groups. The time for acquiring troubled banks passed with two notable exceptions. Not long after my deal was successfully completed, two private investment groups followed my strategic plan. Both groups were formed by past and present US Secretaries of the Treasury: William Simon and Steven Mnuchin.

At the closing of the NDB sale to Shawmut, I received Shawmut shares of equivalent value. Shawmut sold out to Fleet Bank and the Shawmut shares were transferred into Fleet stock. When Fleet merged into Bank of America, I ended up holding Bank of America stock. The Bank of America dividend was so large that I broke the number one rule about investing: diversify your portfolio. I held 120,000 shares of Bank of America at $50 per share in 2008. In 2009 I held 120,000 shares of Bank of America at $2.50 per share, a paper loss of $5,700,000. It has taken 10 years to recover half that loss.

Fortunately, the well hasn't run dry. 200,000 shares of Bank of America had been sold and reinvested while the stock was still selling above $40 a share. In 2012, after attending a luncheon meeting with investment advisors at the Palm Beach City

Club, I stepped into an elevator. I was preceded by a gentleman attending to his wife in a wheelchair. I recognized the man to be Bill Seidman.

Facing the front, I asked, "Is there anyone here from Dartmouth?"

He, wearing a broad smile, introduced me to his wife, saying, "Dear, this man must be among the richest men in South Florida."

I said, "Bill, should I apologize for having made a good deal?"

Holding my arm, he said, "Craig, if you didn't show up, we'd have to invent you."

Craig Takes Early Leave From Shawmut

By REBECCA COX

NEW YORK — William F. Crai[g] said last week that he is taking early re[tirement] as vice chairman of Shawmu[t] Bank.

The United Mine Workers of Amer[i]ca claimed a victory in Mr. Craig's r[e]tirement from the Boston bank, whi[ch] takes effect at yearend. In a long-star[d]ing dispute with the Pittston C[oal] Group, the union had made an issue [of] the banker's seat on the board of [the] Pittston Co., Greenwich, Conn.

But Mr. Craig, 58, insisted his d[eci]sion was personal and not related to [the] Pittston problem. He will remain a [di]rector of Pittston. He will st[ep] from the bank's boar[d]

Three m[onths]

The Boston Herald, Thursday, July 27, 1989

BUSINES[S]

Council votes to clos[e] its Shawmut account[s]

By JOE SCIACCA

BOSTON city councilors yesterday voted unanimously to yank some $20 million in municipal funds from Shawmut Bank accounts in protest of its ties to the owners of Virginia coal mines.

But Mayor Ray Flynn, rather than pulling the funds, appears to want to use the threatened financial action to influence Pittston Coal Group's tense talks with striking mine workers.

"At this time, Mayor Flynn intends to continue to seek a resolution of this matter through discussions with the mine workers and Shawmut Bank officials," said the mayor's chief aide, Raymond C. Dooley.

Flynn last week visi[ted] Virginia to ex[press] support f[or] min[ers]

ston Coal Group.

The city council, led by Councilor David Scondras, had demanded that Craig take action to help end the bitter 4-month-old strike by 1,700 workers in Appalachian coal mines.

Councilors called for Craig to issue a public statement calling for face-to-face negotiations between the company and mine workers; and to quit the Pittston board if his call was not heeded. Craig did neither.

Instead, in a letter to Scondras, Craig said, "Pressuring me off the Pittston board (is) not in the best interest of Pittston employees," a[nd] that he know[s] has bee[n]

DAVID SCONDRAS
'A right to bargain'

bargain collect[ivel]y in good faith."

raig the es- or

council vote al[so] have a moral con[cern] said hotel worke[rs] President Domen[ic] zotto.

Bozzotto, wh[o] joined other Bosto[n] leaders in support[ing] Virginia mine w[orkers] said he is organi[zing an] effort to get Ma[ssachu]setts citizens to [cancel] their personal Sh[awmut] accounts, "even if i[t means] a Christmas club."

Shawmut Ban[k offi]cials, in a writte[n state]ment, yesterday sa[id the] bank "is not a pa[rt of] the Virginia union d[ispute] and has "no busine[ss rela]tionship" with Pittst[on,] by the city council, [the] bank said.

But United M[ine] Workers President R[ich]ard Trumka called C[raig] a "co-conspirator."

"Mr. Craig and S[haw]mut cannot have it [both] ways — supposedly s[tand]ing to act responsibl[e for] their own backyard w[hile] participating in wholes[ale dis]ruption of longsta[nding] communities in Ap[palachi]a," Trumka said.

The Boston Herald, Thursday, July 20, 1989

BUSINESS

Council pressures Craig into action

By PHIL PRIMACK

[BO]STON City Council order[s fun]ds from Shaw-[mut] [last] week

According to Scondras, Craig will call for a Pittston board meeting to discuss the la[bo]r dispute. Craig pledged to resign his Pittston post if his [act]ions are not acted upon.

WILLIAM F. CRAIG
Calls for bargaining

[y]
t[o]
fir[
thi]
Pre[
T]
work[
Mass]
ernme[
Shawm]
$9.3 bi[
million]
Massachu[
from the]
After M[
Wednesda]
dent of th[
praised the]
social respon[
ties to Pittsto]

"We comm[it to rec]ognizing its resp[onsibilit]y to the commu[nity it serves,]" Mr. Trumka said in a prepared statement.

Mine workers applaud as Shawmut exec resign[s]

By JOE BATTENFELD

A high-ranking official at Shawmut Bank, under fire from labor leaders for his ties to the Pittston Co.'s coal strike, yesterday announced his retirement from the bank.

Members of the United Mine Workers union and Boston city officials who support the bitter strike against Pittston in Appalachia called the departure of William Craig from Shawmut a major victory.

"This is the first crack in Pittston's armor," said Arthur Osborn, president of the Massachusetts AFL-CIO. "It's a shame that it had to come to this, but you can't support Pittston's policies in Virginia and try to wash your hands in Massachusetts."

However, Craig, vice chairman of Shawmut and a 13-year veteran of the bank, strongly denied he was forced to leave.

"I felt badly that the b[ank took this measure,]

Group challenges branch opening; Bank of Boston earnings, p. 33

said Craig, 58, of Concord. "I'm leaving, because I think it's time."

Craig said he intended to continue serving on the board of directors of Pittston, and expressed hope the coal company would be reached.

A number of unions, as well as the cities of Boston and Cambridge, recently took action to withdraw millions of dollars from Shawmut accounts because of Craig's position at Pittston.

Craig recently met with Mayor Ray Flynn and others, but had steadfastly refused to resign from the coal company. Flynn announced yesterday he will take action to remove the city's sanctions against Shawmut.

[T]he action on Pittston

dent of AFL-CIO Local [20?] who organized a pro[test] at Shawmut's he[ad]quarters in Boston. "Our intent all along [has] been to put pressure [on] Pittston to bargain [in] good faith." Other u[nion] leaders doubted Cra[ig's] claim that he retired [vol]untarily.

"I think it's clear [that] Craig caved in to the [pres]sure and we cert[ainly] aren't through targe[ting] him," said Tim Bak[er] the United Mine Wo[rkers] of America. "We wil[l con]tinue to seek justice [for] him."

WILLIAM F. CRAIG
Will stay on at Pittston

Craig said he wa[s not] sure whether he [will] join another compa[ny or] plans to do some le[isurely] investment work.

He said he anno[unced] his retirement at a [meeting] today, but reports [We]nesday, but repea[ted] was not forced out. Craig did say [he was] upset at the a[ction] against him, wh[ich]

City Councilor David Scondras, who originally sponsored the city's action, called the move "good for Shawmut, good

220

COMMENTARY
As Reprinted from The Coalfield Progress • Thursday, July 13, 1989

ch behind coalminers 'struggle for justice'

Sullivan

...end?' I ask myself as the now two-... United Mine Workers of America ...al Group continues. Some local ...d Pittston spokespersons blame the ...f violence, condemn the union as ...ake its members the culprits in this labor ... praying and hoping for a just solution, ...ed about and sympathetic with the ...mine grievances of the miners ... ago in his encyclical letter "On the ... Pope Leo XIII called on Catholics to ...ort the rights of workers, for example. ...wage, for job security, for a safe working ...articularly their right to form unions to ...y and to seek redress of grievances. ...ul II in his magnificent encyclical letter, "On ...mphasizes repeatedly the dignity of work and ...s for the benefit of the human person." ... and not 'man for work.'" ...cs applaud the church's support for workers ...dentification with Solidarity in Poland. We ...supportive here at home when workers have ...and when a strike is conducted peacefully. I ...n the current strike there have been some acts ...t these are isolated incidents in a very harsh,

...dwest Virginia is harsh by any standard. Real ...n in Virginia's Appalachia is above 50 percent ...ment in the commonwealth as a whole is less ... Southwest Virginia has rich natural resources, ...s people live below the poverty level. People lack ...dable housing, schools are substandard; hospitals ...linics are scarce. ... king" in far southwest Virginia. The lives and ...people depend on coal mining. The real tragedy is ...lth of southwest Virginia does not benefit its ...ut much of it goes out of the area. The Pittston ...p, headquartered in Greenwich, Conn., is an ...andlord. It has power and prestige. It makes large ...ampaign contributions to both political parties to ...from local and state government.

Miner Struggles

...other hand, the miner struggles to secure a livelihood ...self and support for his family. His welfare is ...d to the pursuit of profit, to the "bottom line" ...

voiced their deep concern about mine safety. In Richlands I met with miners in their early 50s incapacitated by black lung disease who were unable to receive proper medical care or compensation to support themselves and their families. Near Grundy I went down a deep mine and got a first-hand view of the hazards miners face in their work.

The life of a miner is harsh and dangerous, filled with insecurity and anxiety. Miners' families live with uncertainty and experience hardship. Miners are well paid when they work. The present strike is not for wage increases but for job security, for job safety and for the restoration of health and retirement benefits for retired miners.

Pittston abruptly cut off these benefits on February 1, 1988 when their contract with the miners expired. Company officials maintain that what they did is perfectly legal. The retired miners, on the other hand, see themselves as victims once again of "perfectly legal" inhuman and unjust treatment.

People in positions of power appear to side with Pittston. I'm amazed that our state government ... ... law and order ... state troopers to sout... are maintained, ignor... struggle for justice.

I find it distressi... fine on the UMWA fo... assessed $47,500 fo... death of seven mine... 1983.

Civil disobedie... and moral form of... union members or... object to media re... highlight occasion... a conspiracy of si... denial of human... strike in the first... support from the... of Southwest Vir... Committee on R... Committee of A... their families i... a quick, just re... reconciliation

I conclud... the bishops of... Me." "Dear S... recover and c... The dream o... repressed vi...

SHAWMUT NEWS
EWS BULLETIN

October 18, 1989

...le regret that I report that William F. Craig, the ...ut Bank, has announced his intention to retire. ...icult news because Bill has contributed so ...he merger, which produced Shawmut National ...strength of our credit operations.

...his extensive help as a member of the Senior ...ring his considerable banking experience and ...ork. During his thirteen years of serv... ...t his talents to bear on a wid... ...ding investment portf... ...ate lendin...

Flynn limits deposits from city in Shawmut

By Brian C. Mooney
Globe Staff

The city of Boston yesterday joined several Boston-area labor unions in applying pressure on behalf of striking Appalachian coal miners by using their deposits at the Shawmut Bank for leverage. Potentially, it could cost the bank $65 million if all the unions withdraw their funds.

The unions are taking steps to

tiate face-to-face with the United Mine Workers of America representatives, said Laughlin.

Some 1,700 miners at about 25 mines owned by the Pittston Coal Group have been on strike since April 5. Negotiations through a federal mediator are at an impasse, however, according to UMW spokesman Kenneth S. Zinn.

Craig, who has become caught in the crossfire of the strike, was ...ment yester-...sued a state-...the action by ...the striking ...and has met ...ue.

...iyor's placing ...of Shawmut ...i the city of ...ement said. ...party to the ...ston and the ...rs, and fur-...g relationship ...bank and its ...nue to play a ...Boston both ...i and through ...tions and vol-

...told counci-...e has ordered ...Lee Jackson ...ncreasing the ...ds held on de-

vmut's William Craig Ignores Miners' Plight

Shawmut Customers:
Had Enough of
BIG BANK Insensitivity?

'T IT INCREDIBLE that banks can behave as if ...lly don't need their customers? And don't care ...g about the communities that support them? ...'s your chance to take a stand *against* big bank ...ivity *on behalf of* some people who really need ...pport ...

...take a stand against Shawmut National Bank

most dangerous occupation in order to feed their families and make Pittston a profitable coal company.

Mr. Craig has been in a position to see Pittston cut off health insurance for 1,500 retirees, widows, and disabled miners — including individuals burned and crippled in tragic mining accidents.

And he's been able to see as Pittston squandered coal

Shawmut boycott off as Craig quits

By Doug Bailey
and Bruce Butterfield
GLOBE STAFF

A union-led boycott against Shawmut Bank was called off yesterday after the bank disclosed that vice-chairman William F. Craig had abruptly resigned to take early retirement.

Craig, 58, has been the focus of a boycott against the bank because of his directorship of the Connecticut-based Pittston Co., which was struck volume of 747,000 shares.

port Pittson in Virginia and wash your hands in Massachusetts."

Craig, who joined Shawmut in 1976, said he wants to start a "second career," but delined declined to elaborate. He also said he would not give up his director's seat at Pittston.

"I've been a director th years and it's an interes pany," Craig said. "The un to do what they have to do a to do what I have to do."

Bank officials disputed tentions that its boycott h ajor impact on Shawmut': or example, the bank said Boston still has about $ deposit there despite a lor Boston City Counci ithdraw $20 million from

However, the cities of (nd Somerville also joined t gainst Shawmut along v ther labor unions which

drawn their funds and closed their counts.

"I'm certain we had an impact the bank and that his leaving is connected," said Tim Baker, internatio al representative of the United Mi Workers. "We don't have an exact t

3 N.H. banks reported sold to group led b Mass. banker

By Mitchell Zuckoff
GLOBE STAFF

An investor group led by form Shawmut Bank vice chairman W

Union calls off Shawmut boycott

■RESIGN
Continued from Page 25

Mine Workers of America Ppresident Richard L. Trumka.

Thomas Snyder, deputy director of administrative services for the city of Boston, said the city will promptly lift its $14.3 million held at the bank.

"The mayor hop sends a loud and Pittston's unfair la no place in Americ said.

City Councilor chief sponsor of th draw $20 million f Shawmut said Crai "Good for shawmu for the workers; gc

Craig, however "disappointing" If portrayed as a unic

"You pick your Craig said. "You things are runnin thing's going good health. That's the c er it didn't appea brought about the

alf of N ry, havi ederal re major fa sterday.

to be a eek, wou rd waki

two-ye pillars unity ha

also is e ancial an

FDIC Receives Bids From Four Groups For Five Weak New Hampshire Banks

By JOHN R. WILKE
Staff Reporter of THE WALL STREET JOURNAL

Three banks and a private investor group entered bids with the Federal Deposit Insurance Corp. for New Hampshire's five largest independent banks, which have been on the brink of failure for months.

The bidding is a first step toward resolving the state's banking crisis, which has all but strangled the availability of credit in New Hampshire and helped push its economy deeper into recession.

Bidders included Providence, R.I.-based Fleet/Norstar Financial Group Inc., New England's largest bank; KeyCorp of Albany, N.Y.; and First NH Banks, a unit of Bank of Ireland, insiders said. But bank spokesmen, citing FDIC rules, refused to discuss the bids.

The fourth bidder, a group led by for-

The Craig group's bid includes some shared equity, people familiar with the bid said. The group won commitments for about $54 million from a diverse group of more than 30 individual and institutional investors, including John J. Byrne, chairman of Fund American Cos. and a director of American Express, and Ernest Boch, president of Subaru of New England, a Norwood, Mass., distributorship.

The merged banks would be shrunk significantly, with the FDIC taking on the bad assets and paying a manager—either one of the successful bidders or a third party—to liquidate the bad real estate and other assets held by the banks.

Estimates of the bad assets for the five banks run as high as $2 billion, a huge amount in a state the size of New Hampshire. At a House monetary affairs sub-

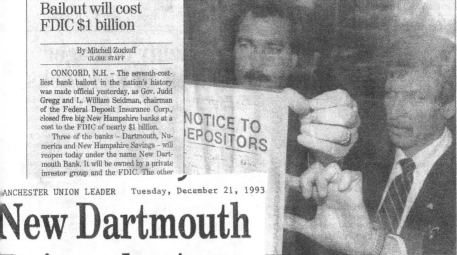

THE BOSTON GLOBE • FRIDAY, OCTOBER 11, 1991

Feds seize 5 N.H. banks

Bailout will cost FDIC $1 billion

By Mitchell Zuckoff
GLOBE STAFF

CONCORD, N.H. – The seventh-costliest bank bailout in the nation's history was made official yesterday, as Gov. Judd Gregg and L. William Seidman, chairman of the Federal Deposit Insurance Corp., closed five big New Hampshire banks at a cost to the FDIC of nearly $1 billion.

Three of the banks – Dartmouth, Numerica and New Hampshire Savings – will reopen today under the name New Dartmouth Bank. It will be owned by a private investor group and the FDIC. The other

NOTICE TO DEPOSITORS

AP PHOTO

...ng sign at the former New Hampshire Savings Bank of-...ore than 100 bank offices closed in the state yesterday.

MANCHESTER UNION LEADER   Tuesday, December 21, 1993

New Dartmouth Raises the Ante

Merger Will Cost Shawmut $170 Million

By TOM FAHEY
Union Leader Staff

The price of New Dartmouth Bank rose yesterday to nearly $170 million when Shawmut National Corp. signed a revised agreement to acquire the Manchester bank.

The agreement extends until June 30, the deadline for completing the merger/acquisition.

The price is climbing as time passes. It will peak at nearly $27 million more than the original price of $143 million.

The original March agreement could have more than tripled the $40 million that investors used to establish the bank in October 1991. The new deal could increase their investment four-fold.

Shawmut had planned to merge New Dartmouth into its operations by Dec. 31, but a Nov.

15 vote by the Federal Reserve Board blocked the March deal. That action reflected the Fed's concerns that Shawmut business and home mortgage programs discriminated against minorities.

Last week, Shawmut reached an agreement with the U.S. Department of Justice and the Fed-...

Shawmut spokesman Robert L. Guenther said yesterday that his organization is determined to make the deal work.

"We're not giving up on it. We think we're in very good shape to stay with it, and we're pleased New Dartmouth has chosen to stick with us, too," he said.

"Obviously, we wouldn't be proceeding with this, nor would the New Dartmouth board, if we didn't think this transaction could be completed."

The original merger deal called for each New Dartmouth stockholder to get $310 in Shawmut stock for each share of New Dartmouth stock. Yesterday, the two banks agreed to a new price of $310.95 worth of Shawmut common stock for each New Dartmouth share, plus 177 percent of New Dartmouth's profits from Oct. 1 until the banks merge.

New Dartmouth has $1.7 billion in assets.

New Dartmouth averages about $1.5 million in net profit a month, roughly $4.5 million to $5 million per quarter. In the fiscal year that ended June 30, 1993, the bank earned $19.9 million.

The new deal," he sa...
"That do...
transaction...
cally when...
agreement,...
doing certai...
The prem...
to the deal...
able for th...
they're aski...
"We're a...
tion than...
year," he...
The M...
was creat...
tober 199...
share. T...
$40 milli...
forming...
hind by t...
jor New...
Numeric...
ings and...
The FT...
in prefer...
Dartmout...
to the ban...
Among...
profit fro...
the New...
system,...

...o discuss layoffs...
...rations. Perhaps...
...close over the...

...ing New Hampshire's moribund economy.

"It's a lot like a serious operation,"...

THE BOSTON GLOBE • TUESDAY, OCTOBER 8, 1991

Group reportedly wins bid for 3 N.H. banks

■ BANKS
Continued from Page 1

Craig's group bid for three insolvent thrifts, Dartmouth Bank, Numerica Savings Bank and New Hampshire Savings Bank, with combined assets of about $2.5 billion.

Still to be resolved is the question of who will take over the state's other two large, troubled banks: Amoskeag Bank, once the jewel of New Hampshire banking but now insolvent; and BankEast, whose parent corporation is in bankruptcy proceedings.

All five were once the darlings of investors, as New Hampshire bank stocks rose dramatically in the mid-1980s with the booming economy. But as the real estate market collapsed, so did the banks' prospects. The state was left with a crippled banking system, businesses were left

damage was done. That apparently was enough to convince regulators to allow him to remain at the helm, sources said.

Less certain is the outcome of the hotly contested bidding for Amoskeag and BankEast. KeyCorp of Albany, N.Y.; Fleet/Norstar Financial Group of Providence, and First New Hampshire Banks, owned by the Bank of Ireland, are believed to have submitted offers for the two-bank package.

Sources familiar with the bidding process said KeyCorp has emerged as the leading candidate, while Fleet/Norstar is believed to have an inside track to manage the pool of bad loans and foreclosed property that the FDIC will inherit when it closes the five banks. A Fleet/Norstar subsidiary, Recoll Management

Hiking with Louise on an Eagles Mere trail.

EPILOGUE (Part 1)

In the spring of 1994, I concluded negotiations with Shawmut for the sale of New Dartmouth Bank. We had very little time to celebrate. That summer, Louise was diagnosed as having well-advanced lung cancer. Dana Farber and Mass General Hospitals offered no hope. She decided to accept palliative care, choosing to be serviced with pain control nursing from her primary physician, Dr. Dennis Berk, with the support of Concord's Emerson Hospital, where I served as a trustee.

We sold the Garfield Road property to Bob Reynolds, the President of Fidelity, and signed a two-year lease on a townhouse in Concord Center, MA. The new address was close enough for us to walk to daily Mass. There was little reason to cook or eat out because family friends and neighbors volunteered to precook and share meals, filling most of our dinnertime calendar. Louise's illness and her need for support were my top priorities. I was fortunate to have succeeded in business and was now free from all office routines. My only aim was to spend quality time with her.

Two of our daughters announced plans that excited their mother. "We want you to plan and attend our weddings," they said.

This was urgent news because they both wanted their mother to share the happiness of their wedding day. Daughter Nancy became engaged to Rich Tobin in August of 1995, and they decided to move up their wedding to December. Nancy and Rich attended Villanova University and had been dating for five years. Daughter Cathy and David Lynch had met after college

225

graduation. They met in Boston and dated for two years. Louise and I got to know both prospective grooms and were delighted with the news.

The anticipation of two family weddings scheduled for December 1995 and January 1996 brought excitement and happy anticipation to Louise. The best painkiller ever. By this time Louise needed a wheelchair and was connected to oxygen.

In December, we took a suite at the Boston Ritz Carlton Hotel, enjoying lunches and dinner parties about town for the week. On Friday, December 29, we attended the rehearsal at the Cathedral, followed by dinner at the Four Seasons Hotel.

The Cathedral wedding required a 60-yard walk up the aisle for the bride and her father. I had already pushed Louise in the wheelchair near the altar. She insisted on walking the rest of the way. Nancy waited for me to return to her at the front entrance. We walked up the half empty Cathedral aisle in step with chamber music. When we reached the front and I peeled back Nancy's veil to give her my blessing and a kiss, her eyes were full of tears.

Louise shed tears of joy when I returned to her in the front pew. All this outward and inward joy continued throughout the ceremony. We were carried by limo to the Algonquin Club for the wedding reception.

Nancy and Rich had prepared for this event by taking dancing lessons. They came down the broad center stairs at the club like Fred Astaire and Ginger Rogers, dancing as the band played, "We Could Have Danced All Night."

Sitting next to Louise, she squeezed my hand and said, "It doesn't get better than this."

Planning for the next wedding began soon after Nancy became Mrs. Tobin. Daughter Cathy was engaged to David Lynch in November of 1995. She thoughtfully agreed to move up their wedding date, as she was eager to have her mother present. We engaged an event planner consultant to handle the details while keeping Louise involved. Cathy chose to wear Louise's wedding gown, which needed little alteration, having been professionally preserved in storage for 38 years.

The wedding took place on January 27, 1996, at Saint Bernard's, our Catholic parish in Concord, MA. The 4 pm Nuptial Mass was presided over by Father Paul O'Brien, who for several years was the assistant pastor and one of Louise's closest friends. There were more than 300 in attendance. Father Paul, a Harvard grad who attended the Gregorian University in Rome, delivered a cheerful homily. He mentioned meeting with and instructing the couple. He said he wasn't surprised to learn that Cathy and David had met in a bar. He asked members of the congregation to hold up their hands if they met their spouse in a bar. Half of those in attendance raised their hands.

After Mass everyone hurried in the rain mixed with snow across the town green to the Colonial Inn for the reception dinner. Louise, assisted by her wheelchair and portable oxygen container, joyfully welcomed guests, as she had done for so many years. When I danced with the bride, I glanced at Louise, seated at the head table, and with a broad smile she threw us a kiss.

Two weeks after the wedding, Louise was taken to the hospital where she spent the last five weeks of her life.

She had been President of Hospice of Boston. She went beyond raising money by visiting cancer patients in the area two evenings a week. She became her own hospice patient, supporting herself by recalling the social and spiritual messages she had previously dispensed to others.

Louise welcomed visitors, who came to witness her prayerful, hopeful attitude. Doctors and nurses, priests and nuns flocked to her bedside to be inspired by her faith. Cardinal Law came to the hospital three times to share her fervent hope for eternal life. Our children and family friends were there most days. Arrangements were made to create a sitting room next to her hospital bedroom, where I could sleep overnight on a narrow daybed. The sitting room furnishings included several chairs and small tables where visitors could collect as a group, allowing Louise to ask for one or two friends and family members to share time with her separately.

Our children made weekly visits. That was more easily said than done. Their ages ranged from 21 to 37. Five were married, living in VA, NC, KS, NY, and NJ. Kids yet single lived in NM, Washington, D.C., and PA. Carrie was in her senior year at Villanova, and to this day Dede has remained in Concord, MA.

Psychologists often refer to a common process when patients are diagnosed with a terminal illness. There is a progression of denial, anger and depression. Louise skipped these phases and went immediately into acceptance.

She planned her own funeral. When Cardinal Law suggested that he would like to officiate at her funeral mass, she told him that it was her pastor confessor's assignment. Cardinal Law was not phased, suggesting he planned to attend the service and would have something to say.

When son Matt offered to write a eulogy, his mother said, "Matt, I'm touched by your loving thoughts, but *no jokes*, and it would warm my heart to know what you plan to say."

Louise's last two weeks of hospital life were filled with conversations that strengthened faith and love, binding the family closer than ever. Her sisters and brothers who could come were there. While morphine and steroids controlled pain and supported her breathing, she was plagued with hallucinations.

She claimed to have seen monsters in a dream, and another time she dreamed she was tempted by the devil.

I was impressed that parochial school training brought out these responses heard from our children.

Dede, who teaches religion classes, replied, "Mom, all your life you prayed to our Blessed Mother for grace and support. The last phrase of the prayer, 'Hail Mary,' says, '. . . pray for us sinners, now and at the hour of our death.' Just keep that prayer in mind."

Ricy had his answer for the hallucinations. "Mom, the gospel mentions that when Jesus ended 40 days of fasting in the desert he was tempted by the devil to turn stone into bread and take a fall off the temple wall to see if angels would protect him. Some theologians believe that Christ was so weakened by fasting that these hallucinations reflected a lack of nutrition and His humanity as well as His divinity."

Louise was inspired, but she also acknowledged that it was sound advice.

Louise slipped into a deep coma. Everyone surrounded her bed and held hands in a prayerful manner. A nurse looked in and reported a phone message from daughter Bonnie. She was at the Kansas City Airport, waiting hours for takeoff clearance while caught in a snowstorm. She was praying to see her mother before she was called by God.

Louise's breathing was weak, and her pulse was difficult to detect. Suddenly life seemed to cease. We sat in silence. Before we could finish an 'Our Father' prayer, she opened her eyes and declared, "What am I doing back here? I felt I had died and was heaven bound."

Someone said, "Mom, we just heard from Bonnie. She has spent the day at the Kansas City Airport stuck in a snowstorm. She has been praying that a flight will get her here before you pass on."

With a faint smile, Louise said, "Isn't God great?"

Bonnie arrived late that night, and while the group at Louise's bedside sang softly, "Up, up and away in my beautiful balloon," Louise died peacefully, March 24, 1996. She was 62. Too young not to see her grandchildren grow up and her husband grow old.

As planned, the viewing occurred in St. Bernard's Lower Church, and the funeral mass was held in the Upper Church. Both were packed with friends and neighbors. Eulogies were offered, including one from Matt and one by Cardinal Law. The service ended at 7pm, and those attending were offered supper at the Parish Hall, across the town green from the church. The next morning, her casket was moved to the Parish Hall from the church, where it remained through the night in front of the altar. At the Parish Hall her casket was placed on a carpet-covered platform, and chairs and tables were arranged around it.

About 150 people joined the family for breakfast, and there must have been 30 people who wished to tell stories about their involvement with Louise.

Pallbearers proceeded to place the coffin in the waiting hearse. Meanwhile, outside, our children passed out colorful helium-filled balloons. As the hearse started on its way to Eagles Mere for her burial, the balloons were released while everyone sang, "Up, up and away in my beautiful balloon."

The following day another funeral mass was said in Eagles Mere for her Pennsylvania friends at the Catholic Chapel located on a property adjacent to Springwood Cottage, a short walk to the cemetery where she was buried. "May she be blessed with eternal life."

Her gravestone is marked with a cross that bears an inscription attributed to the martyred, beatified Salvadoran, Bishop Romero. "I can't, you must, I'm yours – Jesus."

EPILOGUE (Part 2)

Upon the loss of Louise, I soon became aware of how content I was with married life. Perhaps a better word would be spoiled. Indeed, it's a couples' world. It had been 38 years since my bachelor days. Most weekdays were spent at the office with weekends on the golf course. Home meals and chores ad been provided by my spouse, who also maintained the social calendar.

Now I was 65, financially secure, with no wish to establish a new business. When asked about plans, I would reply that I was between deals. I participated with support for some investments, but I backed off taking the lead.

Anticipating retirement, we had sold the condo we used for winter weekends at Quail Ridge Golf Club in Boynton Beach, FL, and purchased a larger house at the Loxahatchee Club in Jupiter, FL. For two years Louise and I planned, and with support from Boston architect Royal Barry Wills, built a large Georgian brick home at the Landfall Club. The property was on a small mound overlooking Howe Creek, north of Wilmington, NC. There was a view across the Intracoastal Waterway, in sight of the ocean. We had our own dock and small boats to take us to the beach and the marina. Louise and I never spent a night together in either house.

Following Louise's funeral, March 27, 1996, son Ricy drove with me to the Loxahatchee Club. He was a teacher at Gulf Stream Academy near Delray Beach, FL. I spent the next two months decorating and furnishing the new Jupiter, FL house, while learning to cook and operate appliances.

In late May I moved to the yet to be completed North Carolina house. After spending a few days at the High Point Furniture market, I was ready to mix and match new stuff with items we had stored at the Concord warehouse. The Landfall house was completed, decorated and landscaped by mid-July, in time to move to "Hart Run" cottage, our Eagles Mere, PA summer home.

The new seasonal rotation was now in place. Eagles Mere, PA for June, July and August – Wilmington, NC for September, October and November – Jupiter, FL for December, January, February and March – and back to Wilmington, NC for April and May, where I kept a 30-foot Grady-White fishing boat at a Wrightsville Beach marina.

Front of "Landfall" home. 613 Dundee Drive, Wilmington, NC 28405

"Landfall" home - Dining Room

"Landfall" home - Library

"Landfall" - Wrightsville Beach Marina- my fishing boat.
Nonpareil getting ready to cast off. Brother
Jack, me, and Jack's son-in-law, Neil O'Keefe.

Jessica Miller

A new love came into my life.

Jessica was born and raised in Akron, Ohio. Her father was a pediatrician, and he founded Akron Children's Hospital. He trained to be a physician at McGill University in Montreal. Jessica graduated from Sarah Lawrence College and received graduate degrees from Fordham and Catholic Universities. While she may have started her education at Our Lady of Elms Catholic School and finished at two Catholic universities, she was Jewish. She married a neurologist, lived in Stamford, CT, and had two sons and a daughter. Her husband, Dr. Resnick, died in his mid-40s in 1979.

She devoted the next 12 years to raising her children and teaching dyslexic kids at New Canaan Academy. In 1992, Jessica married Marvin Becker, an MIT chemical engineer, who developed a successful plastics and chemical manufacturing business with factories in New Haven, CT and Akron, OH. They had a house with a beach on Long Island Sound in Bradford, CT. And they built a vacation home on Cape Cod at Truro on Rider Beach Road.

Marvin died from cancer in 1996 and Jessica went back to teaching at New Canaan Academy. Two of her sisters were members of the Loxahatchee Club. Her mother rented a house there every winter for two months. The sisters married two brothers, Jim and Roger Berk, both Harvard graduates. Jim was a cardiac physician; Roger ran the family-owned TV and radio stations. Jessica shared the Florida house with her mother, Bel Miller.

I met Jessica in mid-winter 1998. It was a Sunday evening and we were both hitting golf balls on the practice tee at the Club. It was around 6pm, and no one else was there. I noticed that she had a great swing. I moved on to the practice putting green, where she also came over to practice.

Years later I prided myself with the memory of the world's greatest pick-up line. "Have we met?"

We exchanged small talk and as the mid-winter sky turned to shadows I discovered that we had much in common.

"Would you care to join me for dinner?"

The trigger was pulled and a delightful relationship followed.

We went golfing together and frequently used her mother's weekly symphony tickets at the Kravis Center. We enjoyed playing tennis, and one morning after an hour of singles, we joined her mother for breakfast. Heading for home, I got back on my bike and when the racket handle slipped into the spokes of the front wheel, I went flying onto the driveway.

Jessica's mother shook her head, and said, "She lost two husbands. Be careful she doesn't kill you, too."

I visited Jessica in Akron and in New York. She came to see me at the Landfall Club. It was in Jupiter, FL where we found most of our common interests. We fished for bonefish in the Keys and explored the Everglades in an airboat. We enjoyed golf when visiting her house on Cape Cod, and for many years we scheduled our time at the Cape to play in the American Seniors Golf Tournament, held at the three best courses in the area: The Hyannisport Golf Club, the Wianno Club, and the Oyster Harbor Club. While Jessica twice won first prize for women, I finished no better than third place.

The relationship was serious when she came to Eagles Mere and met my children. We were on the 16th hole, par 3, up a steep hill, on the Eagles Mere Golf Club.

I said, "There is a reward if you can put your tee shot on the green."

After she hit the ball short, I said, "Try again."

When she managed to put the ball on the green, near the pin, she asked, "What's the prize?"

"Me," I responded, and we became engaged.

Plans were made to marry on November 27, 1999. We arranged for a nuptial service at St. Marks Catholic Church in Wilmington, NC. Father Paul O'Brien came from Boston to perform the ceremony. Brother Jack, who was also living at the Landfall Club, agreed to serve again as best man, and Jessica's daughter Anna was her bridesmaid. The rehearsal dinner was held in our 80-foot long glass enclosed gallery. One hundred guests were served while seated at 17 beautifully decorated tables, accompanied by a six-piece dance band.

The wedding day included a luncheon on board a paddle wheel riverboat cruising up the Cape Fear River with banjos and fiddles adding to the merriment. I was delighted to have my lifetime mentor, Fred Kirby, and his wife, Walker, there. Father Paul's homily was right on target. The reception at the clubhouse was spectacular, especially when Jessica and I were elevated in chairs and waltzed around the room in a traditional Jewish wedding dance.

We took a honeymoon trip to the Turks and Caicos Islands where we enjoyed swimming at the beaches and, on a chartered boat with captain and crew, spent three days fishing offshore. Arrangements were then made to take my nine children and their spouses for an eight-day trip to Ireland so they could get to know Jessica.

Our seasonal routine of PA, NC, and FL now included spring and fall visits to Jessica's house in Truro, MA. This opening and closing of houses went on for 10 years. 2001 was our first full summer together at "Hart Run" cottage in Eagles Mere. Jessica decided that the kitchen utensils could be more accessible if rearranged in different counter drawers. Throughout the summer months my married children came to "Hart Run" for vacations of one or two weeks. Over the course of that summer, three times I heard, "Who moved Mother's kitchen utensils?"

I knew that a large farm with 100 acres of well-maintained fields and woods was for sale. The main house had large windows facing south overlooking the property, and at an elevation of 2000 feet the view was spectacular. From every front window, one could clearly view a series of mountains at a distance of 40 miles without seeing another thing. The house was built in 1955 by Alan Wood, who owned Alan Wood Steel Co. in Philadelphia. His steel mills mainly produced heavy I-beams used for construction of railroad trestles and bridges. The house design was called industrial modern, similar to buildings attributed to Frank Lloyd Wright, having large I-beams for floor and ceiling support, resting on granite columns. We bought the property and named it "Fairview Farm." "Hart Run" cottage was given to my children.

The next five years were spent studying landscape architecture, building design and construction. There was great satisfaction in building stone walls, new roads and trails, and stone bridges. Much of the 1840 bench barn was demolished and replaced or restored, using as many of the hand-hewn beams as possible. We were very fortunate to maintain the employ of John Chestnut, the year-round caretaker, who lived in a house on the place, which we provided. We completely rebuilt and redecorated the caretaker's house. These projects were exciting and required research and professional assistance. Since we were there only in the months of July and August, these projects were on my mind wherever I traveled. I wanted to build a guesthouse beside a large new pond and studied architectural books, seeking the right design, without satisfaction. So I decided to draw my own plans and personally contract out the work. Watching the project through to completion was very rewarding.

"Hart Run Cottage." Front view - deceptively small.

"Hart Run Cottage." Back view - deceptively large.

Daughter Nancy's family on the "Eagles Mere" dock.
Top: Rich and Nancy Tobin with Annie.
Below: Patrick, Nick and Jack

Across from our property entrance was a contractor's barn and equipment yard, including steam shovels, frontend loaders, dump trucks and other machines. I made an offer and purchased the five-acre property, where I directed the construction of a fitness center and playhouse, with table tennis and pool tables, shuffleboard, and a card and gameroom.

Bill's nine children. Top: Matt, Dede, Cathy, Ricy, Bill, Jr.
Bottom: Bonnie, Nancy, Bill, Margie, and Carrie.

"Fairview Farm" - Main House. Muncy Valley, Pennsylvania.

"Fairview Farm" -Breakfast on the Deck

"Fairview Farm" - View from the Path

"Fairview Farm" - Living Room

"Fairview Farm" - Stations of the Cross, one-half mile path.
A great place to walk and pray.

"Fairview Farm" - "The Crucifixion," one of 16 Stations of the Cross.

"Fairview Farm" - "The Resurrection," one of 16 Stations of the Cross.

"Pavilion" - Guest Cottage

"Pavilion" - Living Room

"Pavilion" - Fishing Pond

"Fairview Farm" - Playhouse and Fitness Center

"Fairview Farm" - Inside the Playhouse- Gameroom

Everything was in place for happy living. However, that was not God's plan. Jessica was diagnosed with leukemia. We went back to Boston's Dana Farber and Mass General Hospitals overseen by doctors we knew. We moved into daughter Diane's house in Concord, MA and spent a year receiving reports that her condition was under control. However, in September 2013 her condition rapidly declined, and on October 16, 2013, Jessica died.

I felt deeply depressed and arranged to have her remains transported to Akron, anticipating her interment in a cemetery plot with her parents. A section of Rose Hill Cemetery is reserved for members of the House of Israel Synagogue. Not being a member, I had to join a Synagogue to have Jessica buried with her parents.

As trustee of Jessica's estate, I coordinated the liquidation of her investment assets, including the sale of the Truro house, according to her will. The after tax proceeds were distributed equally among her three children.

Once again I was a bachelor in a couples' world. I soon lost the excitement I had felt when traveling seasonally among four resort houses. The bills I received reflected four golf club memberships and commitments to support an unlimited list of repair shops, hospitals, museums, churches, and theaters, while paying local taxes to four different counties. It was time to shake up this routine and settle down.

I knew I wouldn't miss the Cape Cod house. We were only there for the off-season, part of June and September. I sold the North Carolina house and boat. I formed a family limited partnership for "Fairview Farm", which included a fracking contract for extraction of oil and gas on the property. Ownership of the Fairview Farm Family Limited Partnership went to my nine children at 10% each. I retained 10%, and as lead partner was responsible for maintenance and upkeep.

The plan was to consider Jupiter, FL my main residence and spend July and August at Fairview Farm in the Pennsylvania Allegheny Mountains near Eagles Mere.

My nine children produced 18 grandchildren. Ten grandchildren spend every summer at "Hart Run" cottage with their parents, who have year-round homes within three hours travel time, allowing them to get there on weekends and when on vacation. To accommodate this big group, "Hart Run" was expanded to include 10 bedrooms and a much enlarged, modern kitchen.

Being a full-time resident at the Loxahatchee Club in Jupiter, FL, I sold the house I had bought with Louise and purchased a much larger one, hoping to have family members visit during school breaks.

219 Echo Drive, Jupiter, Florida at the Loxahatchee Club

219 Echo Drive, Jupiter, Florida at the Loxahatchee Club

219 Echo Drive Poolside

219 Echo Drive Backyard Golf Course

Picture of 12 of our combined grandchildren.
Top: Michael Lesaux, PatrickTobin, Brendan Lesaux, Nick Tobin, John
Paul Lynch. Bottom: Quinn Hillingdorff, Kevin Lynch, Maddie Lesaux,
Ellie Hillingdorff, Carter Hillingdorff, Jack Tobin and Annie Tobin

Bernadette Wadsworth

In 2007, I met one of the most beautiful women I had ever seen.
It was such an unusual meeting. We were lined up in the Sunday
evening buffet dinner line at the Loxahatchee Club. Somewhere
between the mashed potatoes and the roast beef and horseradish,
moving right along, I turned and said something that the lady
behind thought was funny. We stepped aside and introduced
ourselves. Her name was Bernadette Wadsworth. I learned that
she was visiting her sister and brother-in-law, Jane and Peter Eby.
I knew them well; Peter was President of the Club. She said she
lived in Toronto, Ontario and gave me her life history.

I can't believe how in such a short stand-up chat, while
holding dinner plates, I learned so much about her. She married
a Notre Dame football star, Michael Wadsworth, in his senior
year. Mike later played for the Argonauts, a pro team in the

Canadian Football League. He earned a law degree while a TV football commentator. Mike Wadsworth was named Canadian Ambassador to Ireland by Prime Minister Brian Mulroney.

Bernadette and Mike lived in Dublin for five years before moving to South Bend, Indiana, where he served as Notre Dame Athletic Director. After five years he returned to Toronto, practiced law, and was nominated for a judgeship. He stepped aside from an appointment, having been diagnosed as a cancer victim. Mike was admitted to the Mayo Clinic where, in the hope for remittance, Bernadette gave him one of her kidneys for transplant. The cancer had spread and he died soon thereafter.

Upon returning to her dinner table, Bernadette was asked by her sister Jane, "What took you so long?"

Bernie said, "I just met someone I could get interested in."

Jane asked, "Who would that be?"

Bernie replied, "Bill Craig – over there."

Jane responded, "Too bad. He would be a good fit, but he recently married Jessica, the woman sitting next to him."

While living in Boston, I became a founder of the American Ireland Fund, a charity raising money for social needs in both the North and the South of Ireland. For several years I served on the committee overseeing the annual fundraiser, a dinner dance in Palm Beach at the Breakers Hotel. Every year I sponsored the event and hosted a table for 10. In January 2014, I wondered about putting together a table for that year's event. Somehow I learned that Bernadette had rented a house at Loxahatchee for the winter. Her sister Jane had died, so I asked her brother-in-law if he would bring her as his date and sit at my table.

He said, "My tux is in Toronto. Why don't you invite her to join you?"

Bernadette Mary Wadsworth Craig "Bernie"

Knowing she had spent five years in Dublin as an ambassador's wife, I was sure we would have a fun table. After asking a mutual friend to find out if she might consider such an invitation, I got the go-ahead. I called Bernie and she accepted my invitation, agreeing to stop by my house the next morning to review the names of the other guests for the table.

She walked over the next morning with her dog, a Yorkshire terrier named Willie, and when I opened the front door, she stammered, "It's you!"

She instantly remembered our meeting years ago between the roast beef and horseradish—or was it the mashed potatoes? We both expressed how happy we were to meet again, and if it were a movie, a full orchestra would be playing exuberant symphonic music.

We gulped down a few cups of coffee, and when I suggested going over the list of names, she said, "Forget it. Let's go to a movie."

We saw *Philomena*, a story about a group of Irish nuns who ran an orphanage from which children were disappearing. Quite a tearjerker. After returning to my home and to Bernie's dog Willie, we couldn't stop talking about common friends and interests.

We were sitting in my study when a phone call came in from a long-time lady friend who I planned to meet for dinner at Buonasera's, a local Italian restaurant in Jupiter. She reported a dental appointment that day for teeth cleaning that resulted in a painful extraction, so she suggested postponing our dinner date. With total belief in Divine Providence, I wished her well, turned to Bernie, and asked, "May I take you to dinner?"

We had an enjoyable dinner at Buonasera's and both of us realized we would enjoy seeing more of each other. Soon we became constant companions. In six months we were engaged. We visited her home in Toronto, then Fairfiew Farm in

Pennsylvania. Both of our families were delighted with the news of our engagement and with our plans for an October wedding in Jupiter at St. Peter's Catholic Church. My brother Jack would be my best man for the third time, and Bernie's granddaughter Madeleine would be her maid of honor.

Wedding photo of Bernadette and Bill. (Far right) Madeleine Lesaux Maid of Honor, (Back left) Caitlin Flynn, Bridesmaid and Ellie Hilgendorff and Annie Tobin, flower girls. Father Stephen McBrearty came from Belfast, Ireland to officiate at the wedding Mass.

Our wedding rehearsal and the wedding reception were held at the Loxahatchee Club, where friends and family members joined us for the celebration, speeches, and dancing. Bernie is a spectacular dancer. You have to see it to believe it. Very few 69-year-olds have that much rhythm and grace.

We enjoyed two cruises during our first two years of marriage. After visiting Paris on our honeymoon, we boarded a riverboat and took a 10-day trip from Marseille to Lyon on the Rhone

River. The following year, after a visit to Toronto, we traveled by ship from Montreal to New York by way of the St. Lawrence River, Prince Edward Island, Nova Scotia, New Brunswick, Bar Harbor, Boston, and Newport. We stayed at the University Club in New York, had our second anniversary dinner at le Bernardin, and flew the next day to Palm Beach.

Soon after returning to our home at the Loxahatchee Club, Bernie was diagnosed as having lung cancer, requiring surgery. The surgeon, Dr. Lee at Jupiter Medical Center, assured us that he had removed all the cancer cells, but after a year of quarterly PET scans, we learned that three small cancerous nodules had returned to her lung.

After an exhausting five months of chemotherapy treatment and three months of cyber-knife radiation, Bernie's radiologist and oncologist reviewed her latest CT Scan report and told us that the cancer was gone.

Fortunately, Bernie's daughter Minnow (Mary) Hamilton was with us at the doctor's office. After celebrating with martinis, she assisted us in spreading the good news.

Our prayers have been answered. We've been blessed. Bernadette is cured.

Bernadette and Bill hiked up Cadillac Mountain at
Acadia National Park. Bar Harbor in the background.

INVENTING ONESELF

ABOUT THE AUTHOR

William F. Craig was born in Philadelphia, PA in 1931, the second son of Irish immigrant parents. He grew up in Upper Darby, a town just west of Philadelphia. After graduating from Villanova University in 1953, he served in the Army Counter Intelligence Corps (CIC). He married Louise A. Haenn in 1958. In 1959 he earned a master's degree in Business Administration from Drexel University while working as a statistician and tax accountant at the Philadelphia Electric Company. At Drexel he wrote articles that were published in the *Public Utility Fortnightly*. This led to an offer to join Irving Trust Company at One Wall Street, NYC, where he became a loan officer in the Public Utility Department. He continued to write business related articles that were published in magazines and trade journals, e.g., *Investment Dealer's Digest, American Banker,* and the *Wall Street Journal*. Irving Trust accelerated his progress throughout the bank. He became Assistant Division Head of the National Division and created an Energy and Mineral Division, designed to finance oil, gas, and minerals production worldwide. In 1974 he became a Director of the Pittston Company, which owned Metropolitan Petroleum Co., Pittston Coal Co., Brinks, the armored car company, and BAX (Burlington Air Express), a worldwide next day heavy freight airline.

Through a headhunter firm he was offered the position of Executive Vice President at Shawmut Bank, N.A., Boston, MA, a 30 billion dollar asset bank. In 1976 he moved his wife Louise and their nine children to Concord, MA. At Shawmut, he oversaw the investment portfolio, Credit Administration, and asset/liability management. He was elected President in 1980 and Vice Chairman in 1984. Bill Craig formed a private equity investment firm, Charter Capital Corporation, in 1990, and proceeded to reinvent himself, buying banks without borrowing any money.

Index

D

E

F

G

O

P

Q

R

S

9 780974 341491